M000291205

midlife, manhood, and ministry

Donald Hilliard Jr.
with Rhonda McKinney-Jones

Andre Price, editorial assistant

FOREWORD BY MICHAEL ERIC DYSON

midlife, manhood, and ministry

The names of all people mentioned in these devotions, including the author's own spouse and children, have been changed to protect the privacy of those individuals.

Bible quotations marked NIV are from the HOLY BIBLE, NEW INTERNATIONAL VERSION®. NIV®. Copyright © 1973, 1978, 1984, 2011 by Biblica, Inc.™ Used by permission. All rights reserved worldwide.

Bible quotations marked NRSV are from the New Revised Standard Version Bible, copyright © 1989, Division of Christian Education of the National Council of the Churches of Christ in the United States of America. Used by permission. All rights reserved.

Cover and interior design by Wendy Ronga, Hampton Design Group.

Library of Congress Cataloging-in-Publication data
Hilliard, Donald.
Midlife, manhood, and ministry / by Donald Hilliard, Jr. ; with Rhoda McKinney-Jones; Andre Price, editorial assistant; foreword by Michael Eric Dyson; afterword by John R. Bryant. — 1st ed.
p.cm.
ISBN 978-0-8170-1729-3 (pbk.: alk. paper) 1. Middle-aged men—Religious life. 2. Midlife crisis—Religious aspects—Christianity. I. McKinney-Jones, Rhoda. II. Title. BV4579.5.H55 2013
248.8'92—dc23

2012034327

Printed in the U.S.A.
First Edition, 2013.

This book is dedicated to my beloved wife,

the Rev. Phyllis Denise Thompson-Hilliard.

Your support, faithfulness, patience, friendship,

loyalty, and unconditional love

have proven to be wind beneath my wings.

I am so glad we made it!

I love you always and forever.

—Donald

Contents

Midlife in Quotes   ix

Foreword by Michael Eric Dyson   xi

Preface by Coach John Thompson III   xiii

Acknowledgments   xv

Introduction   xix

1. In the Midst of Midlife:
The Storm and the Crisis   1

2. Favor Ain't Fair and Painkillers   13

3. Midlife Role Modeling: Biblical Answers   23

4. Father, Family, Faith: Remedying Midlife   35

5. Making a Change and Changing
What We Must   47

6. Pressing Past Pressure   59

7. Shifting Gears and Finding Direction *or*
Ripping Off the Band-Aid   69

8. Forgiveness, Responsibility, and
Restoration—Next Steps   77

9. Where Do We Go from Here?   87

10. May the Circle Be Unbroken   95

Afterword by Bishop John R. Bryant   103

Midlife in Quotes

Beautiful young people are accidents of nature,
but beautiful old people are works of art.
—Eleanor Roosevelt

To keep the heart unwrinkled, to be hopeful, kindly,
cheerful, reverent—that is to triumph over old age.
—Thomas B. Aldrich

Age is whatever you think it is.
You are as old as you think you are.
—Muhammad Ali

When our memories outweigh our dreams,
we have grown old.
—William Jefferson Clinton

You are never too old to set another goal
or to dream a new dream.
—C. S. Lewis

And in the end, it's not the years in your life that count.
It's the life in your years.
—Abraham Lincoln

Aging seems to be the only available way
to live a long life.
—Daniel Francois Esprit Auber

If I'd known how old I was going to be,
I'd have taken better care of myself.
—Adolph Zukor

If wrinkles must be written upon our brows,
let them not be written upon the heart.
The spirit should not grow old.
—James A. Garfield

Grow old along with me!
The best is yet to be,
The last of life, for which the first was made:
Our times are in His hand
Who saith "A whole I planned,
Youth shows but half; trust God: see all, nor be afraid!"
—Robert Browning

A comfortable old age is the reward
of a well-spent youth. Instead of its bringing sad
and melancholy prospects of decay, it would give
us hopes of eternal youth in a better world.
—Lydia M. Child

Foreword

In many ways, he was the true measure of black manhood. Although he was the most famous black man in the world, he suffered great bouts of depression and at times drowned his sorrows in pursuits he knew could only bring him temporary pleasure and fleeting joy. An ordained Baptist minister, he pastored a church with his father while he traveled the globe in search of justice for the oppressed. When he finally gave in to his wife's pleas to own a home, he bought a house in the ghetto where she and their four children were often left alone as he trumpeted his conscience in the troubled land of his birth.

He gave away most of his considerable earnings to the movement for justice he led. He argued with his wife and best friend about how to distribute the prize money for a prestigious peace prize he'd won. His wife understandably wanted him to sock away a portion for the children's future; his best friend figured that, as a companion on the front lines for justice, he deserved half of that prize. The man himself denied both their wishes when he sent every dime to organizations crusading for justice.

He had to borrow money from his father to pay his taxes, and it fell to a friend and follower of means to bought life insurance policies to benefit his four kids in the very likely event of his death. By the time the man died in the shadow of middle age, he'd seen the finances of his organization plummet, his reputation suffer because of his unpopular and increasingly radical social views, and his prominence become overshadowed by an emerging generation.

Most of us will never face the trials and tribulations that Martin Luther King Jr. confronted. Most of us will never grapple with the momentous decisions he was compelled to make in the midst of a fateful struggle for freedom. Most of us will never know the magnitude of suffering he endured as he fought against evil and injustice.

But most of us will face a great deal of what King had to face as he negotiated the treacherous terrain of ascendant middle age. Most of us will deal with the struggle to define ourselves when the world around is crumbling. Many of us will spar with spouses about our finances or battle depression by seeking solace in a bottle filled with alcohol or pills. Most of us will preach some of our best sermons while we combat our worst fears. Most of us will be made hypocrites by failing to meet the standards we proclaim in our pulpits. Most of us will tell our people only what we think they can afford to hear, not realizing that the courage to tell the truth might free them—and us—from our common maladies.

Bishop Donald Hilliard has dared to tell the truth, and if you take what he has written seriously, it may save your life. That sounds like the hyperbole that sometimes flows too easily from religious circles, and yet it's the simple truth. Hilliard has courageously peeked into his soul and permitted us a glimpse of his internal struggles, which mirror our own battles. We need not face everything he faces, or face things in the way he faces it, to learn something profound about how to cope with middle age and the erosions of ego and elasticity it brings.

As Hilliard makes clear, ministers often make hurtful choices that edge us further along the path of self-destruction even as we herald a God who can make a way out of no way. We preach against sexual immorality as we plumb its depths in our own lives, whether embracing stapled flesh on a page or covering our tracks to the strip club. We preach about getting high on the Spirit as we down spirits of inebriation or inject and sniff intoxicating substances into bodies.

Some ministers rail against homosexuality after they've slept with other men, excusing their inclinations as a temporary surrender to evil. They fail to see that the only evil is the failure to be honest about the fact that one can love the same gender and still love the same God who loves all genders the same.

What Bishop Hilliard helps us to see is that we are not bigger than the gospel we preach—what we preach about, and to, others, will be true of us too. Some ministers are tempted to believe that because we are the apples of God's eye that our arrogance won't worm its way into the fruit of our labor. And too often the cold indifference of the kingdom's democracy comes crashing down on our heads when we realize that God's justice rains down on the just and unjust alike. True enough, there is grace and mercy, and the forgiveness of God beckons to us always. But as Bishop Hilliard points out, it is wiser to call on God's favor to keep us from messing up rather than helping us to clean up our mess.

This book is a rich resource for all ministers strung out on the drug of our invincibility. Being close to God sometimes leads minsters to believe we are God. But we're not. God is ageless. We age. God lives forever. We die. God forgives. We often hold grudges. God metes out mercy. We often nurse resentment. God loves beyond merit and desert. We love conditionally no matter how much we say it's unconditional. God is God, we are us—mortal and changing, growing and dying, but wresting life and lessons from the bargain. And God is with us each step of the way.

Martin Luther King Jr. has been a noble paradigm for many ministers. He was a prince among men, a King among preachers. But he also suffered psychic wounds and mortal depression that many of us face as well. We must seek help from on high, like he did, but we must also seek the counsel of trained therapists who can help us face desperate hours when whispers of our mortality speak even more loudly as we age. Of all the great gifts King gave to us, that lesson, drawn from his extraordinary suffering, might be one of the greatest gifts he gave to us. Bishop Hilliard's magnificent book is a powerful inspiration to take that gift to heart, body and soul, and to live as freely and as fully as God intended us to do.

—Rev. Dr. Michael Eric Dyson
Professor of Sociology, Georgetown University

Preface

In his book *Midlife, Manhood, and Ministry*, Bishop Donald Hilliard exposes the truth about the challenges most men face as they approach the middle years of their lives. By the time men reach midlife, we have dedicated decades to establishing our careers and providing for our families. Often we have focused minimal energy in our own personal enrichment. Under such circumstances, as men we sometimes find ourselves in crises. And although this book features men in ministry specifically, its lessons are relevant for men in all walks of life, particularly men in high-profile leadership positions. Spiritual leaders, in addition to coaches, politicians, and business executives, find themselves under pressure to be available to their constituents at all times. Not only is there great pressure to achieve success, but these men often have few, if any, trustworthy mentors to call on when faced with the difficulties of midlife.

I am grateful to have had Bishop Hilliard in my life for more than twenty years. He was my wife's childhood pastor, he officiated our wedding, he baptized our three children, he blessed our home, and he buried my beloved mother-in-law. I have leaned on him for most of my adult life and remain grateful and appreciative of his support, guidance, and friendship.

Midlife, Manhood, and Ministry undoubtedly will serve as a blessing to all men, not just those in ministry.

—John Thompson III
Head Coach, Men's Basketball, Georgetown University

Acknowledgments

Male midlife issues are rarely discussed. Frankly, men rarely talk at all to each other about what ails them. Of course, there are the surface conversations in which we engage, but the "real talk" we really need seldom gets done. I am deeply appreciative and grateful to Judson Press and to its editor, the Rev. Rebecca Irwin-Diehl, for inviting exploration of the topic. Many of my conversations at various church conferences with her involved discussions about our families, and as you will read, one such conversation concerning my youngest daughter led to the birth of this book. She agreed that the combination of midlife, manhood, and ministry deserved real attention. I owe Rebecca a debt of gratitude. We stopped and started this project many times, for it seemed hindered by illnesses of all parties involved and complicated by multilayered schedules that truly defied logic. Somehow, though, we persevered, and the book before you is the result of our labor and diligent work, but also of Rebecca's incredible patience and belief in the need for midlife, manhood, and ministry to be explored.

I would be remiss if I did not thank Mrs. Joan Daily for the transcriptions of the early interviews that served as the initial groundwork for this book. Her attention to detail was critical, and her time was appreciated. And on the final draft of the book, Catherine Griggs, my executive assistant, was a great help in keeping all in the loop as she reread my often-illegible additions and corrections. And for that, I thank her.

There would not be a book at all if the brave pastors from around the country had not shared their stories and their pains, secrets, and struggles. You will not find their names in this book because I promised them anonymity. Each took a tremendous risk talking to me. They pastor churches, shepherd flocks, and are leaders in their communities, but each felt a need to help other brothers avoid pitfalls and find what works and what is worthy of praise. I am blessed because of their honesty. Thank you, my brothers!

Deep gratitude goes to Bishop Walter Scott Thomas of New Psalmist Church in Baltimore for the yearly men's retreat that has become a safe haven for many of us. Much love to Bishop Thomas Dexter Jakes of the Potter's House in Texas for the real talk and the consistent river of deep concern; to Dr. DeForest "Buster" Soaries Jr. of First Baptist Church of Lincoln Gardens, New Jersey, for many years of open conversation and honesty; to Bishop Raphael Greene, Bishop David Michael Copeland, and the late Bishop Otis Lockett, Sr. for decades of holding me up in prayer; to my beloved pastor, Bishop Kelmo Curtis Porter Jr., who baptized, licensed, ordained, married, installed, and ministered to me through my midlife stuff. And I give thanks for Bishop John Richard Bryant, senior presiding Bishop of the African Methodist Episcopal Church serving over the Fourth Episcopal District, by whose hand I was made a Bishop, and who helped guide me through a midlife crisis more than fifteen years ago. I am grateful to all the pastors who have prayed for and nurtured me.

The words on the following pages never would have appeared without the dedication, creativity, and commitment of my editorial assistant, Minister Andre Price, and my editor-in-chief, Rhoda McKinney-Jones. Both of them deserve gold stars for their faithful, sensitive, and careful handling of submitted material and for their extraordinary effort to make sense out of my notes, scraps of paper, tapes, illegible scribblings, and multiple rambling phone calls. Andre's theological overview and suggestions were of deep value. He is a true son in the ministry; he is a part of my family; he is a gifted minister and assistant, and this book would not have been complete without his personal touch and special anointing. As for Rhoda, to her credit, somehow by the grace of God, her incredible talent, and in a manner only she could achieve, she pulled it all together, and what came forth from her hands, I think you will find, is golden. She is truly a blessed and gifted wordsmith, and I am more than grateful to have her on my team and to call her friend.

While writing the book, Rhoda, Andre, and I each had our share of serious physical health challenges and family tragedies. There were days when we almost lost hope, but with prayer, through sheer force of will, and by God's grace, we made it. The journey was tremendous and enriching, and one well worth having traveled.

Here it is. Read and be healed.

—Donald Hilliard, Jr.

Introduction

Children have a lesson adults should learn, to not be ashamed of failing, but to get up and try again. Most of us adults are so afraid, so cautious, so "safe," and therefore so shrinking and rigid and afraid that it is why so many humans fail. Most middle-aged adults have resigned themselves to failure.
—Malcolm X, in *The Autobiography of Malcolm X*, by Alex Haley

Things fall apart; the centre cannot hold. . . .
—William Butler Yeats, "The Second Coming"

It feels like it happened quickly: first seminary, then marriage and babies, pastoring a church, and the stuff of life in between. I was married in 1981, graduated from Princeton Theological Seminary and became a father in 1982, and was leading a church by 1983. I also had become the patriarch of my extended family with my father's death at age fifty-three, and I was just twenty-six. Well-seasoned, I certainly was at a young age. So something always filled the empty spaces of my life—the voices of my children, the highs and lows of ministry, and daily parish life. Then I blinked, and our three daughters had grown up and left the safety of our home for college and marriage and to make uniquely blessed lives of their own. Things quieted, and I struggled with the new mathematical configuration of my family home, reduced now to two—my wife and I. That's when my physical health began to feel the impact of my expanding waistline and a sometimes uncooperative maturing and aching body. When I think about that period of time now, though, maybe things really did not happen in a flash or in rapid-fire succession—the way it actually felt. Perhaps it was more like a steady and persistent march, a not-too-distant drumbeat, an upward climb to what I was obviously becoming—a middle-aged preacher.

Middle age. For some, those two simple words can instill fear. Pastor or parishioner, each us of has the same worries—about longevity, past mistakes, transitions in marriage and parenting, and obvious changes in libido—as well as a nagging longing for what was and what has been. All of us have heard stories from friends about someone in the midst of midlife and the shiny new sports car—the search for the new and elusive something that accompanies the phase. Most of us know what that looks like, for we have counseled friends in the depth of theirs or watched from the sidelines as one struggled through. As I evaluated my own life and ministry, I found it sobering that God, in God's infinite mercy, allowed me to reach this particular place, at this particular time. Many of my family members and childhood friends never made it to midlife, their lives having been cut short by disease, circumstance, and lifestyle choices. So I am grateful and thankful to claim where I am today and to have a modicum of understanding of what it took to get here and to be present.

Why? Because getting to this point has been a journey. And because of my personal experience, I wanted to help other men of faith with their midlife passage, especially fellow ministers, to give them a voice to speak about issues from which most shy away. In my work in the church and with those who bring souls to Christ, I have found that midlife struggles are not necessarily triggered by one particular psychological concern but are caused by various transitions and circumstances from one phase of life to another.

While I am not an expert on the issue, I do know as a pastor and as a man what I have been through, how it has shaped my life, and how it is affecting my future. As I talked to my colleagues in ministry and lay leaders around the country about their own midlife experiences, how they coped, and the solutions they employed, I saw similarities in our struggles. To be honest, I was just glad that I was not alone. Throughout most of our ministries as pastors, preachers, theologians, and lay leaders, we have been striving to reach new heights, build new churches, and bring new committed souls to Christ. Regrettably, however, while empire building we are rarely constructing personal relationships that are fruitful and life-affirming. We are giving ourselves to others constantly and consistently, often trying to be more to our flocks and our friends than God ever intended. So in trying to be faithful to the calling of Christ, many of us neglect our selves and our souls.

I readily admit that my entry into midlife caused confusion, not just for me, but also for those I loved. I had little clue what was happening, so I had no immediate and emotional capacity to fix my particular situation. I felt like I was losing my "swagger," the confident way I believed I moved through the world, that difficult-to-define thing that always had been a part of me. I thought I was losing my "mojo," theologically and otherwise. (Feel free to allow your holy imaginations to interpret that both literally and figuratively!)

So I went to see my personal physician, who talked to me about the dreaded diseases that plague some of us as we approach and pass the half-century mark—hypertension, diabetes, heart disease, and depression, mixed with a detailed conversation about a myriad of emotional, relational, and vocational transitions. Then he drops the big bomb, the one that universally makes all men weep and cringe. He matter-of-factly explains how middle-aged men experience a dramatic drop in testosterone levels during middle age, which may cause changes in sexual performance. Lord, I was not ready for that one. Oh, the joy that "*failed* my soul."

For better or for worse, I was in the middle of a midlife mess. Hopefully, now I am more mature and a little wiser for having gone through a process, with therapy and prayer. In some ways, I am still in transition, and there are still mountains to climb. But for most preachers, midlife can be especially difficult; it is more like the blade of a double-edged sword. Over the past several years, the detailed indiscretions of some popular clergy have made fodder of the personal lives of preachers in the public square. I wonder, though, if there had been someone to whom they could have gone in confidence and laid bare their burdens, would the lives of those men have gone off their charted courses?

The questions before many others and me who try to walk this particular ministerial path are quite simple, though the answers and solutions may be a bit more challenging. To whom does the preacher facing the crises of midlife manhood go to unburden himself about the pains of his marriage, his ministry, or his secret addictions without worrying about losing his congregation, his personal relationship with God, the respect of the greater church community, and the foundation on which he has shaped his calling and his faith?

In an effort to write this book and have it truly speak to the needs of the reader, I interviewed a number of faith leaders throughout the country who were willing to share their midlife stories with me on condition of anonymity (when referring to them in the book, I use pseudonyms). You will not see their names or the churches they represent, or even their church affiliations. They opened their souls and took tremendous leaps of faith that I would treat what they shared with fairness, understanding, and confidentiality. They talked to me for hours about issues affecting their lives and ministries, including their emotional and physical health, the state of their marriages, retirement concerns, addictions to pornography, alcohol, and drugs, the death of parents and birth of grandchildren, self-esteem concerns, infidelity and other sexual temptations, preacher-peer relationships, and changing church politics. They shed their invisible, clerical robes and were bold and brave in their confessions; ultimately, they were transparent in their humanity—mere flesh and blood.

I did not ask the ministers interviewed questions for prurient and sensationalistic reasons. I wanted to get to the heart of their hurt in order to help someone else, for their stories really are not new. They are as ancient as the biblical prophets of old, like the story of David and Bathsheba—sin and condemnation, grace and restoration. Their stories have value and their struggles have merit because all of us can learn from their experiences to develop solutions to better manage our own lives and our own ministries. There is hope, and there is healing. So read the book with an open mind, a receptive heart, and without judgment. Read their stories, relate to their experiences, and reflect upon the wisdom they (and I) have gleaned.

Psalm 51 (NIV)
A psalm of David.
When the prophet Nathan came to him after David had committed adultery with Bathsheba.

Have mercy on me, O God,
    according to your unfailing love;
according to your great compassion
    blot out my transgressions.
Wash away all my iniquity
    and cleanse me from my sin.
For I know my transgressions,
    and my sin is always before me.
Against you, you only, have I sinned
    and done what is evil in your sight;
so you are right in your verdict
    and justified when you judge.
Surely I was sinful at birth,
    sinful from the time my mother conceived me.
Yet you desired faithfulness even in the womb;
    you taught me wisdom in that secret place.
Cleanse me with hyssop, and I will be clean;
    wash me, and I will be whiter than snow.
Let me hear joy and gladness;
    let the bones you have crushed rejoice.
Hide your face from my sins
    and blot out all my iniquity.
Create in me a pure heart, O God,
    and renew a steadfast spirit within me.

Do not cast me from your presence
>   or take your Holy Spirit from me.
Restore to me the joy of your salvation
>   and grant me a willing spirit, to sustain me.
Then I will teach transgressors your ways,
>   so that sinners will turn back to you.
Deliver me from bloodguilt, O God,
>   you who are God my Savior,
>   and my tongue will sing of your righteousness.
Open my lips, Lord,
>   and my mouth will declare your praise.
You do not delight in sacrifice, or I would bring it;
>   you do not take pleasure in burnt offerings.
My sacrifice, O God, is a broken spirit;
>   a broken and contrite heart you,
>   O God, will not despise.
May it please you to prosper Zion,
>   to build up the walls of Jerusalem.
Then you will delight in the sacrifices of the righteous,
>   in burnt offerings offered whole;
>   then bulls will be offered on your altar.

1

In the Midst of Midlife: The Storm and the Crisis

He is the one who will build a house for my Name, and I will establish the throne of his kingdom forever. I will be his father, and he will be my son. When he does wrong, I will punish him. . . . But my love will never be taken away from him. . . . Your house and your kingdom will endure forever before me.

—2 Samuel 7:13-16 NIV

I could not breathe. It felt like I had been sucker-punched in the solar plexus, or like a ton of bricks had been dropped on my rib cage—or something. I just knew I could not breathe. It was August of 2000, and my family was gathered in the college dorm room of our firstborn, the daughter for whom we hoped and thanked God. The unpacking was finished. We had left an emotional chapel service and were about to hold hands in devotional family prayer. I was a complete and total mess. All I could see was what used to be—when she was younger, actually listened, and I could watch over her. I still envisioned her old soccer uniform, our family dinners, and summer vacations in Martha's

Vineyard, where we collected shells and skipped rocks on the beach.

I have an incredible bond with all of my daughters. As a minister who frequently travels, I made a personal commitment to my family and to God long ago to be at the family dinner table at least three nights a week so as not to miss critical moments in their lives, such as proms and recitals. Now this.

I was not ready to let her go. Over the years, our friends shared with us what to expect when children start to leave home. As pastor of a large congregation, I have counseled and coached our Cathedral International members as they prepared their children to leave for college. I thought I knew how to do this. But something about this particular going-away-to-college thing was not sitting well with me. This was *my* child, and I felt like I was on a slippery, downward slide, the beginning of too many letting-goes that were out of my fatherly control. I truly could not breathe.

We bowed our heads and clasped hands. I opened my mouth, placed a hand on my daughter's head, and said in my best preacher-daddy soothing voice, "Lord, cover this child with your anointing." Then the floodgates opened, and I cried deep and heavy sobs. I was hyperventilating, shaking, and not at all prepared for the range of emotions.

On Sunday mornings I preach to those who seek God's guidance. If so blessed, I lead souls to Christ, join couples in matrimony, ask God's grace for those born into the world, and bless the spirits of those departing this realm to join another. I just could not get the "daddy thing" together, though. The empty-nest syndrome had begun, and watching my children one by one go off to college was the final breaking point. It was killing me, and it started a journey with which I still occasionally struggle.

That day in a distant dorm room was, for me, a type of death, and it became my midlife crisis trigger. My story may not be as sexy or as interesting as others, for it was not a tale of a preacher who falls in love with someone outside the boundaries of marriage or a story of a lost minister who absconded with tithes and offerings. My wife and I have had our share of marital crises and struggles. Our life together truly has been far from perfect. But the emotional devastation that threw me into a midlife crisis was grief— mourning of the loss of living children.

In *Passages: Predictable Crisis of Adult Life*, a bestselling and groundbreaking book of the 1970s, author Gail Sheehy laid out in fundamental, practical, and critical ways how midlife affects men and women and the psychological drama and conflicts that often accompany those years. She wrote of renewing the spirit and leaping over emotional and deeply conflicting hurdles to find one's self in an effort to sail smoothly through the passage of middle age. How one copes with those changes of self and/or circumstance, Sheehy wrote, is often difficult and telling.

> Any such change will be painful. A crisis. But not nearly so painful as it is for the man who waits until his forties and bumps into the midlife crisis like a submarine into a reef that wasn't on the charts. The fact that he is locked in only compounds the crisis. Because the forties . . . are a time when it seems no matter what course one has pursued, "everything is turning grey, drying up or leaving home."[1]

My greying hair could be handled more easily than our girls leaving and other home-front concerns. Intellectually,

I understood that my daughters would eventually grow up and find their own way. My wife appeared at ease with this first transition; her story and how she coped is hers to tell. But I was not OK. To be honest, there are days when I still feel the emptiness. As our younger daughters began to leave, I felt a foreboding sense of loss. I was grieving. I missed the family routines and was bothered by the empty chairs at the nightly dinner table. By the time our younger daughter was headed to school, I thought that I was *losing my complete mind*. The silent drive home from her college drop-off was one of the darkest and most depressing days I have ever known.

Part of the challenge has been that my wife and I are very different. She likes quiet; I like crowds. She wants space; I enjoy being surrounded by situations and engaged with people. She handled the launching of our daughters into womanhood with a measure of grace; I did not. So trying to make a new way as a couple, relearning each other's rhythms, navigating and altering decades-old routines, minus our daughters, caused a real and significant crisis in our relationship.

Saying goodbye to our eldest that day was the beginning of many letting-goes and a process of relearning. I shared this and other stories in public, from pulpits across the country, including my own, and in private I confided to male ministerial friends that I was in the midst of a midlife crisis. Congregants and friends alike thought I was absolutely crazy and revealing entirely too much. Many of my colleagues simply could not relate, or at least would not admit to it. There were other pastors, though, who could identify and shared their own stories; they helped me to understand that what I was experiencing did not mean

I had lost touch with reality. Somewhere in the midst of my three beautiful daughters leaving home, I went to see a therapist, for I could no longer deny I was in the throes of some serious midlife madness.

Seeking external help, whether that involves going to therapy, asking for medical advice, or reaching out in general to family or friends, is not something men readily and easily do, particularly African American men and especially ministers of the gospel. Culture, education, and experience have not taught us to ask for help. Men are supposed to bear it all, right? And we preachers hear confessions and the closely guarded secrets of those we cover and attempt to pastor. There is an unspoken rule that preachers are charged with having listening ears but do not share *their* personal pains. So, we do not talk, and we do not expose what makes us vulnerable. In everyday ministry and in real parish life, ministers experience many losses. One therapist told me ministry is like "having someone pick lint off you constantly without replacing the fabric, which leaves you raw and bare."

Truth be told, the whole leaving thing merely highlighted, in bright, glaring, and flashing neon colors, the fact that I was in real trouble, because other life-changing things were occurring. My midlife journey actually began at age thirty-nine, when I started to feel depressed and, well, a little less amorous. That made very little sense to me. I did not know lurking undetected in my body were hypertension and a significant heart problem. I simply could not believe what the doctor was telling me as I went through a battery of tests. It was bewildering and overwhelming to have begun midlife so soon.

Swiss psychologist Carl Jung first identified midlife as a transitional period of soul searching, uncertainty, and examination of self that occurs during our middle years. What he described, though, was not unlike what Sheehy shared decades later. In her book *Passages*, which captivated popular culture of the time and remains relevant today, Sheehy wrote that midlife could be a vexing, complex time of introspection and risky behavior, and, at times, deadly dangerous. In some ways, Sheehy likened those actions and feelings to the darker sides of our humanity and humanness.

> These demons may lead us into private hells of depression, sexual promiscuity, power chasing, hypochondria, self-destructive acts (alcoholism, drug taking, car accidents, suicide), and violent swings of mood. All are well documented as rising during the middle years. The midlife crisis has also been used by psychiatrists as an explanation for why so many highly creative and industrious people burn out by their mid-thirties. Even more dramatic is the evidence that they can die from it.[2]

One young minister I counseled, Jaidon, was totally unaware he was having difficulty until I reached out, engaged, connected, and pulled from him in such a way that he could share his story. "It was a harsh reality to probe my life . . . to help find positive resolve," he said. "The Bishop helped me recognize that the signs of falling into crisis are due to the lack of self-healing and self-preservation. . . . My struggle has always been feeling obligated to people, primarily women, which fueled an appetite inspired by lust, and it has taken years to bridle that and bring it under control."

What often contributes to and complicates the lives of clergy and those in the church is that pastors often feel locked inside their own pain. As a result, some stray from their personal beliefs and convictions. It is "the lack of transparency and the failure to deal with our own struggles, failures, and proclivities," Jaidon continued. "We have lied to ourselves for so long that we have lived that lie before the people and have lost ourselves in what we do. What we do as a profession is the mask that frequently hides who we really are."

Psychological explanations are many for actions taken and consequences given during midlife, but there are also plenty of biblical correlations. Reexamining some ancient Old Testament stories helped me better understand my own struggles and those of the men with whom I spoke. Many come to mind—Jeremiah and Solomon, to name just two. And then there is the need to always have a prophet Nathan–like friend, one who tells you the truth, no matter how it hurts.

Perhaps, if we look at the life King David in the book of 2 Samuel, we can find some answers. God favored David and blessed him, his family, and his kingdom. But David also faced temptations, experienced numerous personal tragedies, and was unsettled. It was in midlife, after battles fought and victories won, that his eyes fell upon Bathsheba—"daughter of the oath"—the wife of another man. David's desire was stirred.

> One evening David got up from his bed and walked around the roof of the palace. From the roof he saw a woman bathing. The woman was very beautiful, and David sent someone to find out about her. The man said, "She is Bathsheba, the

> daughter of Eilam and the wife Uriah the Hittite."
> Then David sent messengers to get her. She came to
> him, and he slept with her. . . . Then she went back
> home. —2 Samuel 11:2-4 NIV

King David was restless and wandering, which left him open to temptation. Many men in the midst of midlife, preachers included, seek affirmation and acceptance, and they start looking to have their egos soothed and assuaged in inappropriate and sometimes precarious places, just as Jaidon, the young minister with whom I spoke, explained.

One study about another Old Testament woman, Delilah, surmised that it was not necessarily her beauty that moved men; it was that she whispered the right things, at the right time, filling a void left by the typical stuff—an all-too-familiar marriage, boredom, stale routines. Midlife is a tender time for most men. Egos are fragile, and insecurities loom large. Though we do not like to show it, we are sensitive beings, and the aging process can begin a traumatic season. Like King David, many of us may be at the top of our games with growing churches and vital outreach ministries, but we are reevaluating the past, regretting mistakes, and hoping for better futures. We are looking at retirement options, managing long-term marriages and ministerial transition plans, and praying that we do not have to preach until we physically drop. We know that tomorrow is not a day promised. Regrettably, no one talks honestly to us about alternatives, safety nets, and escape routes. Then there is this: we are not sure who we can trust to unburden our deepest secrets, such as our King David–like sins.

When I look at King David's adultery, I see that it was not the genesis of his midlife crisis. There were difficulties, evidence of general malaise occurring long before Bathsheba made her grand entrance. What actually was going on in his life? Was he bored? Did he feel empty? Was he lonely? Did he feel loved or adequately affirmed? These are not valid excuses, but they are some of the reasons men often give for wandering outside the invisible but real walls of marriage.

Knowing that Bathsheba was pregnant with his child, and having sent her husband to the frontlines of battle to face certain death, King David repented only when caught and confronted by the prophet Nathan. That is how most of us react; we do not change behavior until we are found out, exposed, because facing our failures, our shadowy sides, can be too painful. King David responds with Psalm 51 and demonstrates the importance of listening closely to one's soul. He tries to get it right.

Here is the blessing in that story: although we are imperfect, God knows our pains and understands our struggles, even if our actions disappoint. Thus, there is always hope and healing for our souls. God is always present, as he was with David. You see, God had a covenant with David. Amidst all his shortcomings and human failings, David tried to cope, rectify, and make good. God promised that David's lineage would always be on the throne. Through it all, God's anointing was on David's head. David regretted his ways and was forgiven for his sins.

> He is the one who will build a house for my Name, and I will establish the throne of his kingdom forever. I will be his father, and he will be my son. When he does wrong, I will punish him. . . . But my love will never be taken away from him. .

> . . Your house and your kingdom will endure for-
> ever before me. —2 Samuel 7:13-16 NIV

Another pastor with whom I spoke, Jaleel, said his personal crisis manifested itself in triple fashion: infidelity,
acute insecurity, and sexual addiction. Jaleel still pastored
his thriving church, but he also feared getting the help he
needed because he did not want to lose his church, his family, or the respect of the greater community in which he
worked and lived. "There always seemed to be a not yet
'accomplished-ness' about me," he said. "I never was rec-
ognized by my peers. I would hear things like 'He's alright,
but he can't preach,' so I never made it on the Hampton
[Ministers Conference] circuit. . . . Then I realized the older
I get . . . my calling is over local ministry and to hear God
say you have been faithful over a few things. That has
become more important than my yearning to hear what my
peers say. That comes with maturity, and I am still working
on maturity."

This preacher's significant anxieties about ministry, his
abilities as a pastor of a people, and his being a man in the
middle of personal transitions led him to engage in the same
negative behaviors about which he had surely counseled
many in his own flock. But Jaleel eventually sought to stem
the tide of the elements that overwhelmed his spirit and
impacted his ability to effectively pastor others. He found a
way to look at himself and face his painful "stuff."

His midlife situation involved not feeling embraced by
peers, and it included adultery and an addiction to pornography. "I still go to counseling for the porn," Jaleel said. "I
now pour all of me into my wife, and our marriage has
gotten better. That has helped me kill the porn and the

adultery [addictions] that were earlier in the marriage. I think all of that came from not being fathered. I'm now learning how to be a father and how to be a husband, and it has helped me to face my demons. It was easy for me to get naked physically, but it wasn't always easy to get naked emotionally. As a growing, mature man, I am now learning how to do that, so there are no more secrets. That's been a blessing."

Not all couples, whether the husband is a preacher or a plumber, survive the trials of midlife. Relational changes are difficult and oftentimes fraught with unfulfilled and unspoken expectations, as I experienced in my own life when my three daughters started leaving home. Their departure left fissures and empty spaces in my marriage that I did not know needed to be filled. Most of one's married life is spent pouring everything into the children, trying to make them whole and productive beings. With the children grown and gone, you might be left with a spouse you no longer know as well as you once thought, and a relearning process must begin.

I readily admit during my period of crisis that I was depressed, wanted to hide, and needed the laying on of hands to pray away the emotional and physical pain. I quickly realized, though, that I would have to find a constructive and practical way to navigate this midlife thing, for the sake of my mental health, my marriage, and my ministry.

I will never forget one Saturday evening when my wife and I were in our bathroom preparing for the Sunday morning service. I was shaving, and she was doing her hair, and we stood at our side-by-side sinks. I looked down, saw something that reminded me of the girls' childhood, and completely broke down—an experience that would be repeated several times throughout that next month. The first two times, my wife held me and tried her best to understand; the third time, she said, "I don't know what to do for you."

Where I was—the state I was in—was a place she could not go for me. I had to find solace for myself and grieve in my own way. I found a path with the help of good doctors, a better understanding of my body and its capacity, a faith in a God who has never left me, and the love of three daughters who have left our home but not our hearts. And so I breathed again, and I tried to help others do the same.

Midlife Discussions

1. What are your regrets in ministry and in your personal life? How did those choices affect you, your faith, and your church community?

2. What are your triumphs and failures? When have you second-guessed decisions that you made as you entered into midlife?

3. Do you have someone with whom you can share and tell your story? If so, who? If not, who might become a partner with you in prayer, compassion, and accountability?

4. What would you do differently, and what would you change if you could?

Notes

1. Gail Sheehy, *Passages: Predictable Crisis of Adult Life* (New York: E. P. Dutton, 1976), 262.

2. Ibid., 358.

2

Favor Ain't Fair and Painkillers

Whatever happens, conduct yourselves in a manner worthy of the gospel of Christ. Then, whether I come and see you or only hear about you in my absence, I will know that you stand firm in the one Spirit, striving together as one for the faith of the gospel.
—Philippians 1:27 NIV

Breathing again can be hard when you are an overachiever. I understand. There seems always a need to have something on my plate—legacy building—maybe to fill the void of missing my children or just a result of having so much early manhood responsibility because of my father's premature death. But as a pastor with multiple ministries, books written, and a shepherd's heart to teach, lecture, and pass the torch of ministry onto the next generation of young preachers, I am forever thinking about next steps and what can be built theologically, physically, and spiritually.

I have not dwelt much on self-preservation until the last few years—my own health and wholeness—though it was needed. But I have thought about the Old Testament prophet Nehemiah and the process of building and rebuilding and how one does that in the presence of enemies, life's daily grind, and personal struggles. What of the midlife transition and what really does come next? Sometimes it is a battle within to regroup and rebuild.

The prophet Nehemiah, as the king's cupbearer, knew a little something about the intrinsic internal and external conflicts of building and rebuilding as he defied opposition to reconstruct the walls of Jerusalem in fifty-two days. In many ways, the task of men in midlife is similar. We have to renovate our lives and restructure our walls during midlife, and at times that means starting over, beginning anew, and occasionally failing until we find what works.

Choosing the right path is not always easy, even for clergy. I have to be honest, not judgmental—just honest. As a bishop in the Lord's church, I have great concern for some of my brothers in the ministry. As the apostle Paul reminds us, we "all have sinned and fall short of the glory of God" (Romans 3:23 NIV). Some of our faith leaders seem to be under incredible pressure and look outward instead of inward to find solutions to their troubles. I do believe we are called to a higher standard, and if we have the faith to confess and seek help, healing happens, and things can only get better. Like the covenant and friendship between King David and Jonathan the son of King Saul, every brother, I fully contend, needs another brother with whom he can honestly talk, freely and openly without a competitive and aggressive edge.

Every brother in and of faith needs another to share his pain and to hear his story while in the midst of a crisis or in an effort to prevent one. That, though, is not how we have been acculturated and raised. As men, we are trained, almost from birth, to compete against one another in the academic world, in the "hood," on the athletic field, and in the marketplace of ideas. We then carry that baggage into our marriages and into our ministries. So when we speak to one another, it is not actually about how God is being faithful, fruitful, and functioning in our lives. Our conversations tend more toward topics such as how many members we have, who is preaching our anniversary celebration, the size of the church's budget, who has invited us to speak where, and if the "right circle" of prophetic preachers has embraced us.

The reality is actually pretty basic. Most ministers go through the day feeling like square pegs in round holes, as many people do. We do not always fit perfectly into the pastoral molds we have designed for ourselves, match the expectations created by others, or have solved the complex riddles of who we are, whose we are, and how we serve. And, we are just too uncomfortable to admit our individual failings and too busy measuring ourselves by the next preacher's biblical yardstick.

Hear this pastor's story as he talks of his personal and professional "perfect storm," the confluence of extraordinary events crashing together catapulting him into a crisis shortly after a parent transitioned. This minister, Jarman, had children leaving for college, a wife who had her own work to do, and a significant church project in the making. None of those issues were in the sphere of his ability to govern, regulate, or control, so he started to spin out of control.

"I came up in a family that was out of control," he said. "Therefore, my response when I became grown was to take control of everything, my environment, my house, myself, my wife, my kids. [With the family member's death] my natural response was to take control. But at that point, I had to admit I wasn't in control. . . . I was functionally depressed. The church was growing, but I was not emotionally or spiritually there. I was preaching every Sunday, but it was angry preaching.

"One time during our men's revival, the preacher was preaching, but it was so hollow for me. Nothing was wrong with his message, but it was hollow for me. I said to myself, 'I don't want to hear this [expletive].' And I walked out and left. The amazing thing is that nobody realized anything was wrong. . . . My whole world was spiraling. . . . This was the first time in my adult life I was alone as a man, and the sisters from the congregation were coming out of the woodwork to 'help' me in any way I wanted."

This pastor, a phenomenal preacher, teacher, and theologian, began to drink, something he did not normally do, to soothe what he could not. "It's possible this was an alcoholic season in my life," he said. "I did not go to therapy or talk to a friend. I couldn't call my pastor because I was the favored son. I was Joseph. How does the favorite son go to his pastor and say, 'Favor ain't fair'? I couldn't tell my church because they needed me to be strong. I couldn't tell my officers because that would put my job in jeopardy. I couldn't tell my friends or colleagues because I didn't really have friends. I didn't have any use for them because I was so busy building. So, all of my friendships were functional. They only knew the reverend doctor and pastor. I realized then that there are some things worse than dying. One of them is at the moment of death to realize you were never truly loved because you were never really known. That changed me and allowed me to begin to be authentically who I am today."

When I talk with ministerial colleagues who are going through rough times such as this, I urge them to bear their "stuff" to a counselor. That is what I did, and I unreservedly recommend it as a first steppingstone on the journey. Whether sought from a fellow member of the clergy or from a professional therapist, counseling may not be the easiest choice, but it is one of the wisest.

In an effort to get through his own midlife onset, another minister, Jericho, told me that he turned to a spiritual director, a faith-based counselor who acts as a guide, to find footing in his life. He felt it necessary to tell his story to someone else in order to heal what he could not see or define.

"My piece was triggered when I finished my doctor of ministry degree and I just felt a void," Jericho said. "Our denomination provides us an opportunity to get some level of counseling. I knew something was wrong [with me], but I didn't know what it was. It was revealed to me for the first time in counseling that I had completed all my education, and once I finished, it left a void. That void was going to be filled with unhealthy activity, I was sure.

"At that point, I definitely knew something was wrong with me and I had to do something. The physical changes—I wasn't working out as much as I used to. The ministry was taking off and doing well, and because of that, I was a little bored. So I filled the void by getting spiritual direction. I have a spiritual director who helps me to see God moving in my life. Spiritual direction has been the best thing that ever happened to me. . . . It has been a powerful experience." Jericho found a path that worked and allowed him to rebuild, reconnect, and restore.

Restoration is necessary for the soul. It is key to being able to make it through any of life's storms, be they the maelstrom of midlife or the whirling dervishes of day-to-day management or the difficulties of church administration. I have had to learn to do things differently, to make better choices about my time, abilities, and my capacity to address what it is I have to get done.

What I know now and what I have picked up along on the journey is that this midlife manhood ministry "thing" will not allow me to do what I used to do in the same multasking, high-tech, fast-paced fashion. I am middle-aged and steadily moving upward, and the climb has made me more reflective, pensive, and tired. Therefore, my decisions are more decisive, and my limitations actually have limits.

Studying, preaching, and pastoring are exhausting—not to mention community work and absorbing the daily pangs and pains of others. I need to take time to pause periodically during the day for prayer, preparation, and the anticipation of what comes next. I need to be able to process and digest events, thoughts, and concerns in smaller segments. I can no longer do late-night assessments of the entire day after focusing completely on church concerns or family issues. I cannot even engage in the rare occasions when I might actually have an opportunity to hang with preacher friends. It's just not happening. Intellectually, I know that to my core. Yet, emotionally I still wrestle with not being consumed by the myriad of problems and pastoral concerns and duties swirling around me. I have had to make peace with finding peace. I learned that going to weekly therapy is a God-sent blessing, not an embarrassment or a statement about my character. No one can or will snatch my manhood card for doing so.

Very early on this voyage I likened my midlife happenings to a woman's menopausal experience—the dreaded "change of life." That made sense to me. I was changing and transforming. Initially, though, I never completely related or fully understood what women experience during menopause or even saw the correlation in terms of what men go through during midlife. Women describe short-term memory loss, uncomfortable hot flashes, loss of energy, and changes in sleep patterns. Men in midlife can relate, though. Trust me: every man can relate. He gets to a particular station in life where he fully recognizes he is entering a transition, or he receives a clear and cogent message from the universe that he is joining the ranks of the elders. Memories do start to fade, and the body is not as responsive as it once was. And yes, the loss of energy can be an embarrassment because it affects libido and sexual arousal. While these changes can be distinctly disconcerting, this time also can be a positive one of reflection and retreat. It can be a time to look directly at the past—mistakes and victories—and decide in what new direction to travel and where that future will lead.

A close preacher friend of mine, Junior, said he knew midlife was approaching when his memory started slipping and his "sensitivity gauge" was on constant high alert. "That was a huge factor for me," he said. "I used to be able to remember numbers easily; now when people give them to me, I have to write them down. Also, now I am more aware of my emotions, and how I'm feeling inside is an important indicator. I am used to having emotional feelings, but they weren't all that important to me. Now I appear to be much more sensitive to what I am feeling emotionally. I even *think* emotionally."

Emotions. Those are tricky things for most men. Somewhere in the universe of statistical data there is a numerical indicator about middle-aged men being suicidal and not even knowing why. Perhaps that is the greatest and most disturbing aspect for men, and for our purposes specifically pastors, struggling with their midlife transitions. We know clearly something is happening to us, to our bodies, our sense of self and how we maneuver through space. What we do not know is how to explain it or how to talk about it, because for most of us it has not been part of our male nurturing, theological training, or maturation process.

I am generalizing, but most women are far more comfortable talking over a cup of coffee about their night sweats than brother-preacher-man is about his tendency to drink too much alcohol or his inability to get a lasting and effective erection. Regrettably, men will simply suffer in silence, sometimes resulting in irreparable and devastating consequences, when in fact there is no need to agonize alone.

One of the ministers I interviewed laid bare almost those exact feelings. This middle-aged preacher, Harcourt, is the oldest but smallest in size of his siblings, whom he raised. He grew up in what he called a "divorced and fractured family" and was always in pursuit of approval and praise, though for him it was an elusive search. He did not find it playing sports because he was not big enough or strong enough. He found it by excelling academically, being the best with words and women, in his fraternity and in his community. Then "God caught up with me . . . and I pursued the gospel track," Harcourt said. Along the way, though, he also developed the complicated and complex habit of "self-medicating with pleasure." In other words, being incredibly sexually active helped him to fill his approval tank and his unceasing need for affirmation and acceptance.

"I think [growing up] I had always been an overachiever, trying to hear the approval of my mother, others, and my peers," he said. "I was not as big as or as fast as my peers, so excelling academically and in speaking were the false pillars I propped myself up on. I never envisioned myself being a mega-church pastor . . . and having experienced instantaneous success gave me the false satisfaction of having arrived. But when I looked around, my peers didn't acknowledge that growth and that success. One preacher told me that my preaching style was nonlinear."

Harcourt needed the recognition of those whom he respected, but he did not feel they respected him and his ability to preach and teach the gospel. So in some ways he had an internal war about his own abilities because he was busy comparing his skill set with others. "I was a square peg that didn't fit," he explained.

"Another preacher helped me understand why I don't fit, why I don't get invited to preach, and why I don't fit in with the clique," Harcourt said. "He said, 'It's hard to be around the authentic when you are inauthentic.' He reminded me that it was OK to not fit. I am just beginning to settle into the fact I am not going to fit and I may not be on the preaching circuit or the televangelist circuit. But I have settled into the call God has given me to be local pastor, and my job is to build up my community and to live out my purpose for my generation. I have finally settled into that, but it has been very hard, very lonely, and very painful."

This minister's midlife struggles stemmed from unfulfilled affirmation as a child. Later on, as a pastor, he found himself looking for approval in what could be called the darker side of ministry, and he pacified and appeased himself the only way he knew how, with secret sexual relationships. Those actions, though, put him in a direct and personal spiritual battle with his beliefs, between what he preached and how he was living. He eventually sought help and made his midlife confusion work.

Although our stories differ, the pain is the same. The Christian men who trusted me with their tales are a group of insightful, talented preachers and teachers who have grappled with their issues but are working on transforming to better their ministries. Each one of them found his own trail. King David wrote psalms, poetry set to music, to ease his pain. I talked through my problems, and I continue to confide and confess what presses on my heart.

I think I will always long for the sound of my daughters when they were young. But things change, and life is not a stagnant, steady state. Emotional and psychological transitions need to be seen for what they are and should not be looked upon lightly. When midlife calls, there are real issues that need attention and answers. We all bear burdens. Bottom line: preacher, prophet, or priest, going it alone is a lonely and thorny road, and one that does not have to be taken. Opening up to another person requires trust, and trust can be hard to come by, for prophet Nathans are few. But they do exist. Finding a level of trust can make all the difference in managing midlife.

Midlife Discussions

1. How have you tried to make your midlife experience work for you? What is your painkiller? How did you confront it?

2. What is your midlife plan? How will you execute it?

3. How has your ministry been adversely affected by your midlife crisis?

4. Who is the prophet Nathan in your life? How has he (or she) helped you to begin your rebuilding process?

3

Midlife Role Modeling:
Biblical Answers

Let no one despise your youth, but set the believers an
example in speech and conduct, in love, in faith, in purity.
Until I arrive, give attention to the public reading of scripture, to exhorting, to teaching. Do not neglect the gift that
is in you. . . . Pay close attention to yourself and to your
teaching; continue in these things, for in doing this you will
save both yourself and your hearers.
                    —1 Timothy 4:12-14, 16 NRSV

In a profession where we ask the faithful to have faith
and believe, ministers frequently have difficulty following our own pastoral advice. On Sunday morning or
during midweek prayer service or in private counsel, we
often talk of "going to God in prayer" and "leaning on
Jesus," but how often are we simultaneously relying on
our own earthly understanding of the theological, biblical constructs and paradigms that have been divinely
given to us? In some cases we, as ordained leaders, are
looking for empirical data, something tangible we can
see, feel, touch, and make sense of when it comes to

grappling with insecurities, our own fallibilities, and crises of faith—those things that make us real.

Earlier I asserted we need to find another brother or sister in ministry with whom we can be honest, before whom we can stand theoretically naked and bear our truths—good, bad, and seriously ugly. We also need something else. Each of us needs a biblical role model: a storied ancient prophet from the sacred text whose life speaks to the core of who we are and the ministries we have attempted to create. We need to fully understand that biblical model's tale, the crisis endured and the lessons learned. So to whom do you relate? What biblical character tells your story?

I have several. Nehemiah is one. It is a story of rebuilding in response to the fervent cries of his people. I relate to Nehemiah because he was moved and responded by acting. He rebuilt the crumbled walls of Jerusalem in fifty-two days despite his enemy's efforts to thwart him. "They are your servants and your people, whom you redeemed by your great strength and your mighty hand. Lord, let your ear be attentive to the prayer of this your servant and to the prayer of your servants who delight in revering your name. Give your servant success today by granting him favor in the presence of this man" (Nehemiah 1:10-11 NIV).

I would like to think I am in tune, in sync, and fully engaged with and for the faithful in my congregation. I am able to work through this particular stage of my ministry partially because I have an image of my time and experience as one constantly and proactively changing to make my life stronger and to help those who surround me.

Ministry, for me, has been about rebuilding, recreating, and remaking in the presence of those who did and do not wish for me to succeed. I always envisioned myself as a person who is willing to change, one who mends, fixes broken pieces, and could reinforce self-created crumbling walls. Sometimes, though, people put everything they have into restructuring and may have to face that all they have worked for may not yield the intended crop. In some ways, that is what conquering midlife is all about: shifting attitudes, making adjustments, recovering, transformations, and, yes, even giant slaying.

Lessons from Moses and Joshua

The story of Joshua and Moses holds a special place in the foundation of my preaching and theological perspective, and it also has grounded me during this manhood transitional phase. You probably know the story already. In his early ministry, Joshua served as second-in-command to Moses, but in maturity he became a dynamic leader in his own right. Joshua was faithful to Moses for forty years, and after his predecessor's death Joshua never lost respect or reverence for Moses.

In recent years, many of the historic African American pulpits have become vacant because their great pastors have either retired or joined the circle of ancestors who have transitioned. There is much talk in the ministerial community about succession planning and preparation for the one who will proceed. The Moses and Joshua story is really one of transition and effective succession. And for me, the key to that story is the crossing and parting of the Red Sea, when Moses, fed by God's power, led the people of Israel, who had been slaves in Egypt, into the wilderness on their way to the promised land. And Joshua, who would eventually stand on the shoulders of Moses, watched the miracle as a way was made and rocky paths cleared as the Israelites charted a course to a safe and sacred space. Joshua then led the Israelites through the Jordan River into Canaan, the promised land. He learned from Moses and leaned on his wisdom.

When things spiral out of my immediate sphere of influence and ability to control, I lean on that ancient biblical story. I do not know where I would be today without the guidance, presence, and patience of the Moses figures in my life. I owe my ministry and manhood to some theological giants. The exodus story reminds me I am not alone in my grief and contemplation because somebody parted stormy seas for me. We all need a theological giant.

I firmly believe I would not be where I am presently if there had not been faithful and guiding hands of those who were Moses figures in my life. There was Bishop Kelmo Curtis Porter, Jr. of St. John Baptist Church in Scotch Plains, New Jersey, where I was baptized, licensed, ordained, and married; Bishop John R. Bryant, Presiding Senior Bishop and Presiding Prelate of the Fourth Episcopal District of the African Methodist Episcopal Church, by whose hand I was consecrated a bishop; Bishop Charles Blake, Presiding Bishop of the Church of God in Christ, Co-Consecrator and friend; and the late Rev. Dr. Samuel DeWitt Proctor, who was my doctoral professor. I mention them here because their counsel helped me then, and leaning on the wisdom they imparted continues to be a blessing today when I am unsure, conflicted, and worried about what comes next.

I stood on their shoulders as I navigated through ministry and through midlife. Their words have been anchors, for I still wrestle with not being consumed by the blank slate of what lies ahead. Moses crossed the Red Sea so Joshua and a future generation could traverse the Jordan River. While they paved a path for us, the blessed "burden" of that gift can also lead to more questions than answers.

Lessons from the Prophets

Many holy prophets struggled with their callings and strayed from the Word of God. But in spite of their challenges and tests of faith, and through their assignments from the Lord, most of them remained faithful to God, waited on God, and were forgiven by God, ultimately making a difference in laying the groundwork for the coming of Jesus the Christ. That simply proves we do not have to stay stuck in our "stuff" or in the constant confusion midlife can cause. The prophets had choices, free will, and so do we. We can move through whatever plagues us, as did many of our elders, and then "run on to see what the end will be"!

The prophet Jeremiah was a good example. Jeremiah felt as though God had deceived him, so he decided he would not preach. There was something within, though, that compelled him to speak: "But if I say, 'I will not mention his word or speak anymore in his name,' his word is in my heart like a fire, a fire shut up in my bones. I am weary of holding it in; indeed, I cannot" (Jeremiah 20:9 NIV).

Then there is Elijah, one of the most interesting biblical prophets of old, who wanted to die because of fear and the weight of his ministry. He thought he failed God in the tasks given. The book of 1 Kings says Ahab had killed all the prophets with his sword, and Elijah, the only one left, feared the same fate would befall him. So he ran and he hid, but God was faithful. Then God appeared, showing up when Elijah needed a word.

> [Elijah] replied, "I have been very zealous for the LORD God Almighty. The Israelites have rejected your covenant, torn down your altars, and put your prophets to death with the sword. I am the only one left, and now they are trying to kill me too." The LORD said, "Go out and stand on the mountain in the presence of the LORD, for the LORD is about to pass by." —1 Kings 19:10-11 NIV

What is more, there is a word of encouragement and comfort for those of us looking back at the mistakes of the past, and it is a word that comes from one of the rare female prophets named in Scripture. Huldah proclaimed judgment against the nation of Judah, but mercy for King Josiah:

> But as to the king of Judah, who sent you to inquire of the LORD, thus shall you say to him, Thus says the LORD, the God of Israel: Regarding the words that you have heard, because your heart was penitent, and you humbled yourself before the LORD, when you heard how I spoke against this place, and against its inhabitants, that they should become a desolation and a curse, and because you have torn your clothes and wept before me, I also have heard you, says the LORD. Therefore, I will

> gather you to your ancestors, and you shall be gathered to your grave in peace; your eyes shall not see all the disaster that I will bring on this place. —2 Kings 22:18-20 NRSV

Then there is the North African Bishop Augustine of Hippo, who chronicled his struggles in his book *Confessions*. He did not flinch from acknowledging not only his chronic wrestling with desires of the flesh, but also his stubborn addiction to the "disease." He confessed, "I was afraid you might hear my prayer quickly, and that you might too rapidly heal me of the disease of lust, which I preferred to satisfy rather than suppress" (*Confessions* 8.7.17).

Great men have been tried and tested, including Old Testament prophets. There will always be another test, a midlife something, another temptation or addiction to battle, another hill to climb, and another form of struggle. The noted Rev. Dr. Jeremiah A. Wright, esteemed theologian, pastor emeritus of Trinity United Church of Christ in Chicago, Illinois, and my brother in the faith and former classmate, frequently says in sermons and to seminary students, "All of us are either in a storm, coming out of a storm, or headed into a storm." There will always be another—something over the horizon headed in our direction. This means we will be tested, tried, and confronted with difficult choices—some that confound, some that tax the heart, but the head knows choices must be made.

Look again at King David. God favored him. "He chose David his servant and took him from the sheep pens" (Psalm 78:70 NIV). Although David was a mighty warrior who slayed giants, had armies at his command, and was a gifted and prolific musician, he still wanted more. But what he wanted was not his to possess. Swiss theologian Karl Barth has said, God's no eventually leads to a greater yes. It was not that God would not give David more; the "more" simply had to be in the right context.

In repenting, David offers psalms, his gift of music. "I waited patiently for the LORD; he turned to me and heard my cry. He lifted me out of the slimy pit, out of the mud and mire; he set my feet on a rock and gave me a firm place to stand. He put a new song in my mouth, a hymn of praise to our God. Many will see and fear the LORD and put their trust in him" (Psalm 40:1-3 NIV). Or, as the seasoned saints of God are often heard to proclaim—those faithful Sunday-go-to-meeting church folks—God may not come when you want him, but God is always right on time.

Identifying a Role Model of Your Own

In my interviews with those in the faith, one pastor, Hamil, told me of the numerous biblical influences who helped him cope. Leaning on God and the stories of the prophets helped him come to grips with the alcoholism that worsened as he dealt with the growing changes in his body, the decreased testosterone, which altered his sexual responsiveness, and the insecurities and jealousies threatening his ministry and marriage. He needed the ancients' fortitude to work through the complexities that plagued him. What Hamil experienced, though, was similar to how most men feel as they approach the middle-age milestone. It is exactly how I felt—desire, ability, frequency, all that—but everyone's pain is expressed in a different manner. Not better, not worse, just different.

"I was always athletic," Hamil said. "So the trigger for me with midlife was when that was gone. I thought I was going to be able to do that even when I went into the ministry. I identified with my physicality, so when I turned thirty-seven and I couldn't do what I used to do, I began to spiral. The other challenge for me has been a jealousy of my peers in the context of ministry. I compared myself to those I really like and love. Not being celebrated by them, I compared that to my physicality as well, and that was a real challenge for me.

"So my story really is with alcohol, and that began to be a fight again. That began to be part of the physical issue, not being able to stay in the moment longer sexually, and the alcohol seemed to help. . . . The challenges for me have been revisiting the alcohol. . . . But my openness to talk about it has helped my wife and me. My marriage is a great marriage now. . . . I could have this conversation if she were sitting right here, right now."

My own midlife journey left me with many more questions, and the answers at times were painfully slow in coming. Who am I now at this point in midlife? Who am I to God? Who is God calling me to be in the future? How am I to change my ministry to be more effective, productive, and present to the needs of the people and my needs as a man, husband, and father? Questions—the prophets of old had them too. And I know all the ministers whom I have encountered over the years have pondered the same.

Because I am so thankful for and to those who plowed tempestuous and tangled fields so I could walk through untethered, I now see myself as a Moses mentor, a ministry coach, a pastor who guides and directs Joshuas, not only through the blessings of ministry, but also through their doubts and insecurities of manhood and ministry as midlife approaches.

I am not alone in connecting my personal story with that of Moses and Joshua and other prophets of that day. Another pastor, Homer, said,

> I think, biblically, there is a lot to be learned from the names you mentioned. I followed a pastor who had been at our church for thirty-three years, and I got our church to a particular place. I was able to step in and take the mantle and lead the church to the next phase. . . . I learned from Joshua how he respected and always honored the Moses before him. . . . I think all key leaders, no matter where they are in life, have to take their hats off to those who cut bushes down on the path they are now walking on. Joshua models that well.

Personally, I have also identified with Timothy because most of my ministry has been "cutting edge" and progressive. When I entered the ministry thirty-five years ago, I was able to experiment with my pastorate and how I decided to lead. The apostle Paul consistently implored Timothy, his spiritual son, to remember the things that he had been taught. Paul's desire was for Timothy to find a right path, to not make the mistakes that others had made, and thereby to avoid making a shipwreck of his life and his faith. He was to guard his beliefs, to guard his life and his faith. It was good advice for the young church leader, and it remains wise counsel as we age and mature. Guarding what we believe and relying on lessons learned can be helpful tools as we work our way through pains, secrets, and the process of rediscovering self in midlife.

Midlife Discussions

1. Who is the biblical role model in your life? What lessons or insights have you gleaned from that person's story in Scripture?

2. Who has been your real-life Moses? How has that person functioned to help you with ministry and with manhood?

3. To what extent have you relied on your Moses or role model for encouragement, accountability, challenge, and comfort?

4. What challenges do you see in the future? How will you navigate them?

4

Father, Family, Faith:
Remedying Midlife

Be completely humble and gentle; be patient, bearing with
one another in love. Make every effort to keep the unity of
the Spirit through the bond of peace.
—Ephesians 4:2-3 NIV

My father died too young—in midlife, as a matter of fact,
at the age of fifty-three. I am not sure he had an opportunity to experience all the transitional changes, the joys and
pains this period can bring. His death and his life, what he
stood for and how he raised me, were preparation for this
journey. Losing him when I was only twenty-six years old
was more than devastating, so his passing made me reflective about what I have achieved and created. His death and
life may be why family is so important to me and why my
daughters' departures, coupled with my own critical health
issues, sent me into an early midlife whirlwind.

In *Passages*, her classic work on midlife, Gail Sheehy
wrote of a man with similar sentiments I have about my
children creating separate lives and not needing me as much
as I needed them. I truly was grieving the loss of those who

were very much alive and were happy and extremely well-adjusted. Then my therapist added a new dimension to understanding my midlife experience. At the time my "nest" was emptying, I was also nearing the age of my father's death, and subconsciously I probably was concerned about the potential of my own demise. Could I successfully exceed that benchmark and productively thrive? My therapist advised I would feel some angst until that time passed. There was truth in theory. And so I worked. I worked hard on myself trying to find a balance of what was satisfactory and what was not. I threw myself into my ministry and relationships that mattered, and I focused on family.

I have learned that the love and support of family can be a crucial factor in helping someone through the tricky passage of moving through one stage of life to another. I love my family, and that was a tangible and precious gift my father gave, taught, and demonstrated for me through his everyday living. So the love I demonstrate for my wife and our grown children, what they give back and pour into me in return, has made some of my darkest and troubled days much brighter. However, it has not always been easy. It never is.

I recently wrote in a tribute booklet honoring my father, acknowledging that at his death he did not leave me riches or the financial seeds for generational wealth, but he gave me a good, solid name, an abiding faith, and the knowledge of what it means to be a man of honor and integrity. He gave me a foundation on which to build and the tools to weather difficulties when tempests toss. I try. There are days when I fail, fall completely down, as we all do, but my dad showed me how to get back up, how to work, how to think and to process my way through "the troubles." I do try. I like to say my father left me a legacy of virtues as opposed to vices.

As I said in the introduction, family struggles and complications, especially for men of the cloth, can be like the "blade of a double-edged sword"—dicey. For there is the public face of ministry and the private, internal pain of whatever is troubling the spirit and whatever is making a situation sick. The pressures of the ministry gift can take a tremendous toll on our psyches and our emotional well-being; and so there are times we wear invisible masks, cloaks to cover and hide hurt and imperfections, using anything to conceal that which might cause worshipers to question our calling to serve Christ. Marriage, parenting, and making a family function take hard, persistent work and continued sacrifice; and though we counsel others on how to conduct themselves and how to manage their lives to make circumstances better, we do so knowing our own fallibilities, the cracks in our God-given natures, and that we do not always get it right in our private dwellings and personal relationships.

One truly anointed pastor, Hugo, for whom I have a tremendous amount of respect and love, opened his soul and told me about the enormous conflicts that at one time plagued his marriage and physical health, and that ultimately threw him into a crisis of faith and deadly suicidal thoughts. He questioned whether God had even called him, had given him the gifts he possessed, and if he would ever set foot in the pulpit to preach the word of God to his congregation again.

"I was truly suicidal," Hugo said when we talked. "They had to put me on suicide watch. All I could think was what in the world was I going to do now. I couldn't preach and I couldn't teach, and it turned me into a very mean person. It made me a negative person. . . . I stopped reading. I didn't want to touch the Bible. I didn't want to talk to anybody about the Bible. That was a major crisis for me. Then to have as a result of that a relationship, somebody outside [marriage] who I felt could understand. It was my mind playing tricks on me, but it felt good to have somebody else who I thought could understand what I was dealing with. My situation awakened some of my dark areas. I thought I was beyond anything like this happening. . . . It gave power to a lot of my weaknesses. I like women, but I've always been smart enough to know when to walk away—until this happened. When this happened, I said to hell with it. I might as well live for me."

Hugo added, "People were checking in on me, but it was a dark time. It made me understand how some people reacted to me when I went to minister to them and they would say, 'I don't want to hear all that.' It helped me realize where people can be emotionally when they are going through things. People were calling me, but I just really didn't want to hear it. I never talked to a therapist through all of this. I should have, but I didn't."

Thank God this young minister moved past what had him bound in a significant crisis. The mere fact he felt like he could not share his pain is a clear indication of why it is imperative for pastors to have another pastor who can and will counsel in confidence.

I have known pain as well, the kind that comes from lack of communication and missed intimate connections. I have been there in my own life. I understand those struggles, and I understand how husbands and wives, men and women, process their "stuff," their sorrows, differently. When my wife's mother passed in 2006, I took the wise advice of a good friend: I could be there for my wife and love and hold her through her struggle, but coping with that particular loss, as I did with my father, was a place I could not go with her. She had to go it alone, on her terms and in her unique way. No one knows or comprehends until they have their own encounter with unspeakable pain.

In my years of preaching, teaching, and trying to bring dedicated souls to Christ and to demonstrate the love of God, I have experienced so many losses, from devoted members who transitioned, to the internal and everlasting church politics that seem to never cease. Nearly every year around Holy Week a Judas steps forward. Something ugly happens. Someone leaves the church, or a negative letter or email curiously finds its way into my hands or onto my desk expressing some form of dissatisfaction. That has affected and affects me, and it can make an impact on my midlife experiences.

My pastor's advice was to continue to love the Lord with all my heart, to pray without ceasing, and to make daily praise and hard but good work a steadfast lifestyle choice. I have worked as a pastor all of my adult life. Hard work and focus have sustained me through some treacherous times and kept me out of difficult situations—trouble. Working hard has taught me responsibility, and it has become the corner-stone of my ministry and the legacy that my father left me. Work is a blessing from the Lord. Remember, God created the heavens and the earth in six days. After each day, God evaluated and analyzed what God had done and called the creation good. That illustrates to me that God has a divine work ethic, and that hard work is what we are called to do.

I tried to follow my father's example by filling the imprints left by my daughters' departures. I redirected some of the energy I once had put into my daughters on a daily basis into my many sons and daughters in ministry. I tried to counsel them about what I was experiencing and how they could be better pastors to their people and avoid pitfalls. I became more active in the life of the church, but more selective as well. Then I started seriously plotting a constructive succession plan. I want the person who succeeds me to have a solid theological foundation but also a shepherd's heart. I planned conferences on religious topics geared toward self-improvement. And finally I took my own advice by learning to care for my health and well-being. I had to pace myself and eliminate the unnecessary.

Yes, my father (and mother) instilled in me by word and by deed the importance of rising each day and being productive, filling my days with constructive acts. He always had two jobs and worked harder than any man I have ever known. I cannot remember a time in my childhood when he did not provide; and my mother worked just as hard. My father woke up early and came home late, and we never felt neglected. The Bible describes Job as a righteous man who suffered greatly, but he sanctified those he loved and would awaken at the day's dawn to tender burnt offerings for all his children. He was a responsible man, despite all his trials. He waited on the Lord and was of good courage, and God strengthened his heart. Midlife was challenging, but I, too, have been known to wait on the Lord.

In Paul's second letter to the Thessalonians he said, "For you yourselves know how you ought to follow our example. We were not idle when we were with you, nor did we eat anyone's food without paying for it. On the contrary, we worked night and day, laboring and toiling so that we would not be a burden to any of you" (2 Thessalonians 3:7-8 NIV). In this particular letter Paul had to deal with believers who refused to work. They had become idle in their conduct, leaving themselves open to life's temptations.

Hard work. I have done my best to honor my father's life, to take up that mantle and make home a safe harbor for my family. It is a place, I pray, where love and warmth are in abundance. My father's actions made us feel secure, nurtured, and loved. He was a living example of what it means to make an effort and how to make a difference in people's lives.

I remember clearly being in my twenties after graduating from college and simply wanting to take a brain break. I was exhausted, and I thought taking a moment was a reasonable request. I was tired and needed rest, so what could be the problem with a time out? It was not going to be a permanent thing, just a temporary moment to regain sense of self and sure footing so that I could make adult choices about my future. Again, I thought I was making a somewhat reasonable request. My parents did not, and they made their dissatisfaction clear. They said I had two days to sit at the kitchen table while I looked for a job. My rest was minimal at best, and so I went to work.

It was not unreasonable to ask of a healthy, college-educated, twenty-something young man. Now, however, I am long past twenty, and I cannot move with grace and ease. I know my limitations and my capacity to give. Midlife is upon me, and though vexing at times, it has made me not just older, but also much wiser.

The wisdom of good, hard work that I gleaned from my father—each lesson was a great one. This has sustained me through bad times and given me a solid foundation, and so

I believe I have an obligation to pass it on to those who come behind me. Jesus said, "From everyone who has been given much, much will be demanded; and from the one who has been entrusted with much, much more will be asked" (Luke 12:48 NIV). Nothing has given me greater pleasure than to pass on the concept of good works and to hand down joy and a sense of accomplishment onto our children and my sons and daughters in ministry.

Persistent work can fill voids and vacant spaces that ministering to people sometimes brings. Pastoring is a never-ending job, one with great rewards and some very low lows. That is precisely why I tell those whom I cover and watch over in ministry, young men and women who have been called to preach God's word, to always make family the top priority and to place them before their congregations, and then everything else will follow, fall into line, and find a proper place.

For some, the concept of family may be difficult and fraught with multilayered issues and complications. I well understand not everyone grew up in a relatively drama-free home such as mine, with two solid parents. I have been blessed. Sometimes, however, the histories that we carry forward from our families of origin are lessons in contrast. I recently spoke to another minister who told me that it had been his responsibility to throw away his father's multiple liquor bottles, and he vowed he would not be like him, and he would be a better father.

Even with familial conflicts and disappointments, ultimately it is those we call "family," whether biological or created, the people who consistently show up and support you, are the ones who will be with you in the end to help fight battles and dodge the daggers you never saw coming.

I can hear the voice and the words of Rev. Dr. Claudette A. Copeland, co-founder and pastor of New Creation Christian Fellowship, as she says, "Pastoring a church is like pastoring a parade." Rev. Dr. DeForest "Buster" Soaries, senior pastor of the First Baptist Church of Lincoln Gardens in Somerset, New Jersey, likens pastoring to being at a bus stop. "People come in, get off, and move on," he says. You have to be prepared for those changes in your ministry context. They are inevitable. Family can make such transitional stages of ministry life positive and not a season filled with pitfalls. They can make midlife manageable. Find a way to lean on them.

I have found that part of my calling is to share what I know and mentor young pastors and ministers in training. I work hard and find great satisfaction in knowing that I have impacted someone who has been blessed with theological gifts. I counsel, converse with, and caution them when they begin to pastor their own congregations, telling them to be compassionate and caring but not to get their hearts too connected, entwined with, and attached to those whom they minister. Some people are not in your life permanently; they are there only for a season, and seasons change, shed their leaves, and grow anew. I tell them to watch the changing seasons, the people, and be willing to accept that although one's methodology may have to change, the Christian message remains untainted.

Ministry has changed drastically during the years of my pastorate. I have to make changes for the church, for my family, for my community, and for my own sense of self. Right now, I have six young ministerial charges currently seeking personal counseling and therapy to help them learn how to navigate their pastoral waters. I preach and plead with them to part willingly with some traditions so that they can chart new paths and build on new ideas, which may bring unexpected opportunities into their lives.

At some point in midlife we have to make choices and reach beyond our comfort zones to explore and expand our territories. We have to make a choice along the way to be happy and hopeful. While at times hope is an elusive thing—or as the nineteenth-century poet Emily Dickenson said, "Hope is a thing with feathers"—at many times it may be the one and only thing that we can grasp. I say walk in hope, lean on the One whom we serve, and make a conscious decision to be happy, even on your most difficult days. Make a concerted effort to make another person happy, decide to reconnect with your wife or with the parent with whom you refused to speak for the last five years. You may pass some days without drinking water or eating significant sustenance, but you cannot live meaningfully and purposefully without hope.

What did the old hymn writer pen?

> My hope is built on nothing less
> Than Jesus' blood and righteousness.
> I dare not trust the sweetest frame,
> But wholly trust in Jesus' Name.
>
> On Christ the solid Rock I stand,
> All other ground is sinking sand;
> All other ground is sinking sand.
>
> When darkness seems to hide his face,
> I rest on his unchanging grace.

In every high and stormy gale,
My anchor holds within the veil.

Manhood and ministry are divine responsibilities. Fatherhood is as well. When circumstances shift, age creeps, the weight of ministry falls heavy on our shoulders, and midlife confusion knocks repeatedly at our doors, we have to act and make an effort to move through the process. God made us in the divine image, and we are supposed to be instruments through which God's promises are fulfilled. God is a father to the fatherless and a mother to those who know not a mother's love. Abraham was the father to Isaac and Ishmael and the natural father to the entire nation in the spirit (Genesis 12). We are to be spiritual navigators on holy seas, but we cannot be the people God intended if our rudders get stuck on shore and we cannot see through shallow waters to get to the clearing on the other side. Hope does indeed spring eternal, and hope, coupled with hard work, can make manhood and the complications of midlife bearable.

Midlife Discussions

1. Over what circumstances or people in your life are you grieving?

2. Identify any negative ways in which you are handling the shift. What can you do to turn that negative into a positive?

3. In what ways are you preparing for additional changes in the future?

4. What lessons can you carry from the past into your future? How does your family history inform your present choices?

5

Making a Change and Changing What We Must

Therefore, I urge you, brothers and sisters, in view of God's mercy, to offer your bodies as a living sacrifice, holy and pleasing to God—this is your true and proper worship. Do not conform to the pattern of this world, but be transformed by the renewing of your mind. Then you will be able to test and approve what God's will is—his good, pleasing and perfect will.
—Romans 12:1-2 NIV

Change is never easy, whether it is changing one's mind, attitude, heart, perspective, or even one's current longitudinal and latitudinal location. Change just is not that easy. The New Testament tells us that "Jesus Christ is the same yesterday and today and forever" (Hebrews 13:8 NIV), but we are to be transformed (Romans 12:2). Changing, shedding past hurts, beginning anew, and choosing the suitable road to travel, whether well-trod or newly paved, is what we are asked to do as Christians. In the Old Testament God said to Joshua, "Do not be frightened or dismayed, for the LORD your God is with you wherever you go" (Joshua 1:9 NRSV). The loving presence of God does not and will not change, but we must be transformed in an effort to become whole in the body of Christ. The apostle Paul wrote, "Listen, I tell you a mystery: We will not all sleep, but we will all be changed" (1 Corinthians 15:51 NIV).

The concept of stasis—remaining in a singular, unchanging mode—at times is good, especially if things are going well and the trajectory is positive. So why change? Well, that is easy to answer. If we are to climb the rough side of midlife's mountain, we must be willing to change, alter plans, do things in another manner, from modifying our lifestyles, how we work and manage our churches and families, to planning for the future to finding a simple hobby. We have to make changes in an effort to make a difference, to stay relevant and relatable, so we can truly speak to the needs of our people.

A number of years ago famed gospel musician Walter Hawkins, now deceased, made popular the song "Changed," which spoke of the transformational love of Jesus Christ. During its time this song was sung by every African American gospel choir and in black churches across the country. Even today, every so often you may still hear it on a gospel radio station, the choir or soloist crooning about the change that has come over the one who has been saved by Jesus—a wonderful change that has liberated and restored that person to wholeness.

That is what happens in midlife—change. In fact, midlife is the ultimate definition of change. And I believe that it is time for men, and for ministers of the gospel in particular, to look at our lives as if standing on a high hill. It is time to take a sincere inventory of our accomplishments, taking stock of all we have done and all those whom we care about, family, friends, and our faithful, and see clearly and squarely what is behind us, where we have been, and the sacrifices made. Yet, we also need laser-like clarity to visualize what is ahead, the untapped opportunities and experiences, and willingly develop new navigation systems, the necessary tools, to get safely where we need to go and not get lost. The hard part is figuring out what that is and in what directional pull one should lean. One thing is certain: new roads will need to be plowed, and fresh ideas will need to be explored.

Easier said than done, I know. But it is important to spend time contemplating what comes next. What is happening in your church? What is truly important to your congregants versus what you personally desire? Do you delegate more responsibilities to your staff, and how are you preparing for a fruitful future? Many of us are so psychologically and emotionally entrenched in our physical places of worship, fully consumed by the next church campus building phase, and the sparkling brand-spanking-new worship center—that sacred space formerly known as a sanctuary—that we forget about the stages needed personally to make our daily lives more complete and balanced. Do we simply slow down and exegete the gospel until it is apparent no one is listening, or do we have a reasonable transition plan in place to pass the preaching baton to that young, talented, well-trained minister who is right on our heels sprinting beside us? So what does come next? And how do we get there?

Those are all good questions, ones with which I have grappled with for many years. A number of pastors I interviewed have also given thought to those very notions and freely talked about next steps, solutions, their current emotions, and how they are adjusting and readjusting to personal physical changes, aging, the shifts in capacities to complete a given duty, and all the stuff in between.

A pastor whose story I shared earlier said of his middle-age period, "A new me is emerging. It's related to recognizing that there is an episcopal call on my life. There is a call to mentor pastors. And I have struggled with this. Whenever I am around young pastors, they gravitate toward me. They even write to me on the Internet and don't even know me.

"Second, I realized I could actually have a life outside the ministry and outside the church. That was when I first began to talk about retirement. In our bylaws we have a pastoral transition piece, and this has now defined my priority at the church."

Another pastor shared that it was imperative that he made different choices about ministering to his flock and managing his daily pastoral duties. The profession of pastoring, as I have mentioned numerous times, is a blessing in a divinely wrapped package, but it can also be all-consuming if one does not set a pace, find a rhythm that works and is productive. We cannot be all things to all people, even if we would like to, and too many of us try to do so.

In midlife we begin to recognize that there are mounting limitations on our physical capacities and abilities to engage in tasks that we once did with ease back when we were young preachers possessed of new, devout energy and theological enlightenment. Accepting that midlife reality can be extremely disconcerting, however. Many of us are ill-prepared to handle the emotional, spiritual, and psychological trials of transitions, be that midlife or church-related, because we are not taught as men, in youth, or as pastors in seminary how to find workable solutions. We do not always imagine ourselves beyond our calling to the pulpit, and we cannot visualize our pulpits filled and our churches led by another.

Hear this pastor's story. Hakeem understood that change was necessary in order to maintain and grow his ministry. "In my pastoral duties, I am changing a number of things, including the number of direct reports I have," Hakeem told me. "I have been reducing those numbers over the years. I have nine direct reports now, and probably before the end of the year that will be reduced to three. I am managing the affairs of the ministry through staff, which is a critical thing. If I have to get some things done, it will be done by one of those three people. . . . I don't do counseling anymore; I used to do a lot of counseling. Now, I do limited counseling, special situations and leadership.

"I had a health crisis a couple of years ago, and as a result the elders in my church have given me a week every month to rest. I preach four services on Sunday, and with the Tuesday night Bible study and managing everything else, they thought I needed a week off, Monday through Friday, to do whatever I want to do. I still work during those days . . . but I have the freedom to go away, refresh, regroup, think, play, or do whatever I want to do. That's been huge. It has played a critical role in relieving my stress. . . . Stress creates all those diseases, and so that week off has been life-changing."

Yes, change is hard, but if done with contemplation and planning, it also can be rewarding. Even revered, ancient religious leaders questioned their callings, their futures, their actions, and their harbored doubts about how to move forward in faith. In his *Confessions*, written between the years 397 and 398, Augustine of Hippo spoke of his internal conflicts before his conversion and how he struggled to find the peace that the Lord gives, which cannot be measured and passes all human understanding.

> In my own case, as I deliberated about serving my Lord God, which I had long been disposed to do, the self which willed to serve was identical with the self which was unwilling. It was I. I was neither wholly willing nor wholly unwilling. So I was in conflict with myself and was dissociated from myself. The dissociation came about against my will. Yet this was not a manifestation of the nature of an alien mind but the punishment suffered in my own mind. —*Confessions* 8.10.22

Augustine wrote about what I often think and search my soul. Who am I now that I have reached this middle passage? And who is God calling me to be in the future? I have said that I see myself as a mentor, one who covers and teaches not only what it is to be a man, but also what it takes to be an effective pastor with meaningful reach to those seeking solid relationships with Christ. I spend a lot of my time working with the pastors in my church and those for whom I am responsible as a bishop in the faith. I frequently lecture on pastoral self-care and talk about what we need to do so that we don't feel like we are losing our souls and salvation while saving others.

I tell young preachers that every pastor needs space and time to regroup, reflect, and talk to God. Every pastor needs to create boundaries and rules with parishioners and for themselves so they do not become tangled in a web of uncomfortable and uncompromising positions. We are ministers serving a great and glorious God, but we are also human beings, flesh and blood, as well. In my book *Somebody Say Yes!* I wrote that pastors live in a world "where our problems are great, and our stress level is so high we are easily tempted to find rest, refreshment and respite in all the wrong places. Sometimes we become so tired that we yield to an allusion of safety. Once it is too late, we find that this safe haven is a trap."[1]

I also encourage my charges to be open with the prophet Nathan in their lives to unburden what has them bound. Then I give my charges in ministry the wise counsel that my therapist has given to me: "Give people all of God, but do not give them all of yourself." To always give the unwavering, unconditional love of God is important, but no one should give all of who they are. To do so is draining and ineffective for clergy and unproductive for congregants as well as their pastors.

In my twenty-nine years of pastoral ministry, I have had incredible experiences and blessed opportunities, so I feel an obligation, as I get older, to embrace the Moses who I have become and is innately me—a ministerial coach and spiritual guide. The Lord has been faithful to me, and I want to pass on that cloak of knowledge to others. I acknowledge fully that the Lord has allowed me to walk through doors that have swung on welcomed hinges, but I always left the doors ajar so that those coming behind me could step through easily. That is what I see in my future and what I work toward.

In my ministry I have participated in the Oxford University Roundtable and preached at the prestigious annual Hampton Ministers Conference, and I was a student of one of the greatest theological minds of our times, the late Rev. Dr. Samuel DeWitt Proctor. God has also graced me with the occasion to exercise my preaching gifts in some of the greatest institutions and pulpits of the twentieth century. I want to be able to share those experiences with the many men and women I have commissioned in the ministry and with new ones on the horizon. Those are my future plans, building on the past to pass it on. In order to make those personal goals a priority, however, I have had to make conscious decisions to slow down, reassess staff and preaching engagements, and learn the art of delegation. Yes, we must plan to change, but often the first step is for a change to come over us.

"I love Timothy, who followed the specific structure given to him by Paul," one minister, Jafari, said to me. "I learned from studying him that to build a successful organization you need people who are faithful and dedicated enough to take the organization to the next level. Make their responsibilities important to them. Paul says to Timothy, choose from among you those who have demonstrated faithfulness. . . . If I want my ministry legacy to last, I need to pick people who have demonstrated faithfulness over a season . . . and those are the people who I pour into."

Gail Sheehy suggested in her book *Passages* that refocusing goals and ideals is a significant course of action to get through the challenges one faces during midlife.

"You must give up believing that all the riches of life will come from reaching the goals of your idealized self," she wrote. "If your ideal self is evidently not going to be attainable and you refuse to adjust down, you will go the route of chronic depression."[2]

Sheehy was not implying that we should limit our aspirations; she was simply imploring those who have incredible goals to be realistic about capacity and ability. Failing to do so leads to depression and intense feelings of insecurity. Realism is key, and learning to be grateful at whatever stage we have reached is important to embrace so that we can move forward and not "get stuck on stupid and parked on dumb," as the old adage, says.

"My declining health was a sure-fire indicator that I'm not young anymore," one minister, Adwin, told me. "I used to pride myself on how well I could see and my ability to go out and rip and run and do things. I can't do it anymore. I cannot work sixteen-hour days; I just can't do that anymore. I used to be able to go to bed at one a.m. and get up at six a.m., and it would be no big deal getting four or five hours' worth of sleep. I simply can't do that anymore either. And my memory is not what it used to be. All these are indicators that I'm aging."

While the word *change* really defines midlife, so does the aging process. And we have to be able to accept where we are in our ministries, our bodies, and our personal lives. We are changing; that is a fact. The reason I wanted to put pen to paper and write this book was to bring pastoral midlife out of the closet and into the light. As men, we fail to talk with others about what pains us. Instead, we run and hide. We abuse alcohol, watch pornography, overindulge in food, look outward instead of being introspective, or we simply bury ourselves in work at hand. Or we will overwork, over-build, and overtax ourselves because we do not have the skills to communicate. Preachers, yes, human still, we just bear our multiple scars in secret.

In this season we should be trying things we have never done, traveling somewhere we have not been, and scheduling the time to do it. One of the ministers I interviewed actually flies airplanes as a hobby. We just have to be vulnerable enough to extend ourselves and reach beyond that which makes us comfortable. We cannot pastor our flocks if we are failing, flustered, fatigued, and falling apart. We need sacred healing and the courage to train for the future today. While learning to embrace alternative options, we must utilize the power and practice of prayer and praise. The psalmist says, "I will bless the LORD at all times; his praise shall continually be in my mouth" (Psalm 34:1 NRSV).

In moments of anxiousness and doubts about what is next in the current landscape of ministry, make a commitment to pray and praise consistently, and without pause. The Lord will show up and show out and point you in the right direction. That is a guarantee.

Midlife Discussions

1. Obviously, as we go through midlife, we cannot hold on to what we had in our twenties. In what ways are you letting God reposition and transform you in the midst of your changing context?

2. What things are you doing to shed old stereotypes and images of your manhood in order to manage your current changing emotional, psychological, and physical state as a seasoned pastor, husband, and/or father?

3. What new things are you trying that you have never attempted before? What new gifts and new hobbies is God revealing to you in this season?

4. How have you changed your diet as your body changes physiologically?

Notes

1. Gail Sheehy, *Passages: Predictable Crisis of Adult Life* (New York: E. P. Dutton, 1976), 262.

2. Ibid., 358.

6

Pressing Past Pressure

Therefore, since we are surrounded by such a great cloud of
witnesses, let us throw off everything that hinders and the
sin that so easily entangles. And let us run with perseverance
the race marked out for us.

—Hebrews 12:1 NIV

Although the mass exodus of our daughters prompted my
midlife experience, it did not stop there. My story in many
ways is and remains no different than others. An uncontrol-
lable snowball reaction was in full effect. In my home and
at church one issue would arise, then another, and another,
and somewhere along the way, I simply lost count. There
are no medical quick fixes or vaccinations to ward off an
infectious case of "the Christian troubles." As a pastor, I
have had no immunity to marital challenges or disagree-
ments with my children. I speak often of my extraordinary
wife and our three beautiful daughters, but our adult children's departure from our home left a void, a vacuum, and
a vast disconnect. What we went through hurt and left fes-
tering wounds that took time to heal. We had to get beyond
what had us bound so we could press past the pressure.

Another pastor I interviewed, DeMarcus, shared the
struggles he was having in his marriage. DeMarcus had

been coping with the possibility that his wife had been unfaithful, and as a result he was not completely convinced he wanted to remain with her. They had simply drifted apart. According to DeMarcus, she made clear that being married to him was not necessarily her agenda. The idea of a possible affair left him reeling, feeling insecure and inadequate. He was worried about church members hearing of possible indiscretions in his household, and he struggled to find balance. How could he minister to them if they knew about the troubles he was having at home?

"She didn't want to be married to me anymore," DeMarcus said. "I was never home, and she just wasn't in love with me. I probably should have stayed in therapy following my marital issues because that did something to my confidence I have never recovered from.

"I've not gotten past it. We do well . . . I think a lot of my emotional ups and downs are because I have not been able to let it go. It was a very dark period for me."

Although I had not experienced this pastor's particular plight, I understood the pain of which he spoke. He needed counsel and a healing word. His hurt was palpable, and his confession to me was raw; however, he was receptive to the possibility that things can and do get better. In that moment he was Joshua, and I was Moses and knew just a little more "something" about pastoring, church drama and dynamics, family conflict, and the full emotional commitment to and for one's spouse. He had been open, and so I needed to let him know he did not walk alone.

As I have said before, and I will say it here again, every pastor—everyone who is working through issues, for that matter—needs a therapist. And forgiveness is key, for whatever the transgression, major or minor. We have to assess and understand our roles in a given situation, and in order for healing to take place we must then forgive our partners and ourselves. Forgiveness is a two-way street.

I have preached in hundreds of churches and heard countless pastors speak to their people. They speak of hope and God's infinite ability to forgive. They speak of social ills and the injustices of the day. They speak of gifts of the Spirit and the "wonder-working" power that true faith brings—the amorphous entity we cannot see but feel. There is, however, nothing like listening to a seasoned saint of God, an anointed old-timer, who rises from his "preacher's chair" before the day's sermonic reflection, purposefully walks toward the center lectern, and from deep within, like an uncontained spiritual rumbling, utters in a resonant voice the poetry of an ancient standard hymn. He recites something like this, from George A. Young's "God Leads Us Along":

> In shady, green pastures, so rich and so sweet,
> God leads His dear children along;
> Where the water's cool flow bathes the weary
>   one's feet,
> God leads His dear children along.
>
> Some through the waters, some through the flood,
> Some through the fire, but all through the blood;
> Some through great sorrow, but God gives a song,
> In the night season and all the day long.
>
> Sometimes on the mount where the sun shines
>   so bright,

God leads His dear children along;
Sometimes in the valley, in the darkest of night,
God leads His dear children along.

On those days, I know without a doubt that I am a child of God, and God carries and guides when valleys are too deep and my feet will not go *"another further."* Our God does protect his children. We need that assurance during life-altering changes and challenges. We have talked about transforming and climbing over roadblocks stacked in the way of successful pastoring and nurturing our families in such a way we do not make them our excuse not to reach greatness. We can achieve nothing if we are unwilling to confront sins, personal vices, insecurities, and those daily crutches on which we lean and that claim victory over our lives.

We have to face our metaphorical and physical demons and fight for solutions through counseling, twelve-step programs, religious retreats, and true meditation with God. For this reason, I attend a yearly Arizona-based men's only retreat held by Bishop Walter Thomas of the New Psalmist Baptist Church in Baltimore, Maryland. He brings together a variety of pastors, preachers, and theologians to discuss numerous issues involving the church and our personal lives. In a relaxed atmosphere and manner, we congregate at tables on a daily basis to talk, share, confess, and look to solutions for our lives and church struggles. Each spring, I also hold a gathering called the Safe Harbor Conference to provide a space for pastors to decompress and find deliverance from their issues. And I am also on the board of the Samuel DeWitt Proctor Conference, Inc., one of the fastest-growing, ecumenical social justice organizations in the country. Each February we gather, men and women, to talk about a myriad of issues concerning "the church" and its politics and to seek solutions for our congregations, our communities, and ourselves.

Getting honest and asking for help is not an easy undertaking for African American men who are not used to being vulnerable. We have to get real, face facts, and find workable, sustainable solutions, or we will lose the blessings God has granted. We all have "stuff" and have gotten drenched during stormy seasons. How we get through the rainy days to find solace and a sense of peace to reach the other side is what makes us successful and is a testament to and of character. That is real change. And it takes emotional and spiritual maturity.

As I said in a sermon at the Progressive National Baptist Convention, we must "press past the pressure." Practical solutions to complex preacher problems—I have just a few answers and a couple of insightful suggestions. As men of the gospel, we have to help our community, the African American community, and ourselves, really, to demythologize depression and psychotherapy. We have to press past our fears of getting honest with ourselves. Then we must pray faithfully and powerfully so that if medication is recommended, we may avail ourselves of that remedy as well.

In an interview, another preacher, Malik, said, "That piece [the need for honesty and for outside sources of help] must be taught in the black church. Black men, more so than black women, are not given to getting help. That is why so much of what we do is destructive. Women will get together and cry about it and talk about it. Men, we go inward, which can lead to alcoholism and other destructive behaviors."

In the convention sermon I reminded the preachers about David's story in 1 Samuel 30:1-8, before he was king and when he returned from sixteen months in Philistine territory. He was close to being sent to war against Israel, but he and his men were dismissed because the Philistines feared their allegiances. A defeated David returned to Ziklag to find it in ruins and his wives gone. The army turned on him because he had not left the city secure and protected. They talked of killing him, which scared David. "David was in great danger; for the people spoke of stoning him, because all the people were bitter in spirit" (1 Samuel 30:6 NRSV). Then David sought the Lord and inquired, "Shall I pursue this band? Shall I overtake them?" And God answered David, "Pursue; for you shall surely overtake and shall surely rescue" (1 Samuel 30:8 NRSV).

David felt enormous pressure, but he pressed past what ailed him, gave pause, and leaned on God's word. There are so many external forces pushing on us daily. There are home pressures, marital tensions, car breakdowns, a weak economy threatening job security, empty church coffers, kids' sports events, increasing debt, stubborn congregations, and environmental concerns. The weight of everyday life can be overbearing. Internal stresses and external pressures are some of the most disabling factors hindering success. They do not come to us one at a time, but instead like grapes on a vine—in a bunch altogether. The goal is to develop a strategy on how to pick and eat each grape, one at a time. It can be a true trial and test of will.

Then there are pressures caused by things missed, that could not be envisioned and anticipated, like the downward spiral into alcohol after the loss of a parent, or a spouse who found solace and excitement in the arms of someone else. The apostle Paul did say, "For our struggle is not against flesh and blood, but against the rulers, against the authorities, against the powers of this dark world and against the spiritual forces of evil in the heavenly realms" (Ephesians 6:12 NIV). We have to gain the strength of David and press forward and not get stuck in things past. As the apostle Paul also said, "Brothers and sisters, I do not consider myself yet to have taken hold of it. But one thing I do: Forgetting what is behind and straining toward what is ahead, I press on toward the goal to win the prize for which God has called me heavenward in Christ Jesus" (Philippians 3:13-14 NIV).

David felt dismissed and disregarded—betrayed. Many of us feel that way at work and at home. There is a unique kind of burden and tension a shepherd experiences in trying to manage a flock, all with its various needs. The pressure felt is often the result of those exact people. But what would we do, and who would we be without faithful members? They can be hurtful, harmful, and haughty at times. But these are the very people whom God has called us to serve and to love.

Again, it is fine to give people all of God, but do not give them all of yourself. David had a similar dilemma, but he altered his perspective and went to the Lord about those who were contentious and difficult. His army was looking for a scapegoat, not solutions, but David inquired of the Lord. Many of us need a temporary change of venue to gain sure footing.

Here is the blessing I discovered in my walk: if you brush your shoulders off (to steal a line from Hip Hop mogul Jay-Z), dismiss haters, stay away from those who abuse power and your heart, and shift attentions, better days will come, and God will show up. God did not place us here to die under the weight of pressure and problems. God helps us when we are in the middle of trials and self-created dramas. God created us on purpose for a purpose. German Reformed theologian Jürgen Moltmann, in *Theology of Hope*, talks about the tension between the times. There is tension between the promise and the manifestation. David gives us a solution, a remedy for this present age. God heard David and answered his call. In the midst of storms we need to remember that we, though ministers of the gospel to others, need the healing word of ministry for ourselves. If we call on God, the Lord will answer.

Was it not David who said, "But you, O LORD, are a shield around me, my glory, the One who lifts my head high" (Psalm 3:3 NIV)? David also said, "Even though I walk through the darkest valley, I will fear no evil" (Psalm 23:4 NIV). In Psalm 27:1 David said, "The LORD is my light and my salvation—whom shall I fear? The LORD is the stronghold of my life—of whom shall I be afraid?" (NIV). And then in Psalm 61:2 David prayed to God, "Lead me to the rock that is higher than I" (NIV). If we lean on God, the Lord can lead us through ministry pressures and personal pains. And then, sometimes we have to lean on one another, ask for help, and pray for strength, but ultimately we have to encourage ourselves.

Gospel artist Donald Lawrence sings an appropriate and fitting song entitled "Encourage Yourself." The words speak to living through life's difficulties and pressing past the mark. And the lyrics also evoke another Scripture about David, who, in a time of trial and trouble encouraged himself in the Lord.

Midlife Discussions

1. Because people can be a major source of your pressure, what healthy ways do you have in place that allow you to distance yourself?

2. David encouraged himself in the Lord. Who or what encourages you?

3. Many times pressure can leave you feeling "dissed" by those closest to you. As a leader, how clear are you on your role and responsibilities so that you do not become a "people pleaser" in order to avoid negative feelings?

4. What mechanisms do you have to build yourself up in pressure situations? Do you stand in the mirror and talk to yourself? Do you declare the word of God over yourself?

7

Shifting Gears and Finding Direction
or Ripping Off the Band-Aid

Therefore I do not run like someone running aimlessly; I do not fight like a boxer beating the air. No, I strike a blow to my body and make it my slave so that after I have preached to others, I myself will not be disqualified for the prize.
—1 Corinthians 9:26-27 NIV

For men, and pastors in particular, mastering middle age requires many adaptations and shifts in thought, but it ultimately warrants trying to find a steady state in which to live and work and have authenticity. My father blessed me in numerous ways, but part of the important legacy he left upon his death was an understanding of the necessity to give back, personal responsibility, accountability, and teaching what has been learned and passing it on to the next generation. It would be selfish, then, not to reach out, extend myself, and share with brother preachers what I know, starting with self-preservation, solidifying one's course, and releasing the fear to be great.

As fathers, preachers, and teachers, we have a divine and ancestral obligation to never let mediocrity reign. Nowhere is this truer than in the African American community. Too many black boys believe survival is not possible past young adulthood. They cannot see that joy dawns in the morning. They have lost hope, and in some ways it is understandable, if all that is projected before them is negative and degrading. Many adults, parents in particular, are tightly wedged between tragedy and a hard place, attached to their pain, lamenting shattered dreams and missed opportunities. With increased age and wisdom, we are called to be role models, better leaders, more attuned listeners, and gentler spirits, but that can be accomplished only if we first bandage our own injuries, accept our position on the journey, and reclaim the hope we have lost.

Rev. Dr. Gardner C. Taylor, that formidable minister often known as the "poet laureate of American Protestantism," wrote in his book *Faith in the Fire*: *Wisdom for Life*: "Hope is joyful and conquers the wistful spirit. It faces our trying days of unbelief and cold practicality with a magnificent If, the mightiest Maybe, and a grand Perhaps. This is hope and it exists outside us and beyond this life. This is the incurable optimism that flows like a spring from the human heart."[1]

So, how do we as middle-aged male pastors find center, the hope we have misplaced, and discover meaning and acceptance without losing our souls? Many men I interviewed said for them, it started with unadulterated honesty, ripping the Band-Aid off destructive appetites and allowing fresh air to flow over open wounds. Talking about difficulties, developing practical action plans, establishing pastoral transition strategies, and recommitting themselves to their families and to Christ, were sure starters. Perfection, of course, is not on this side of glory. But the desire to do better and be better was far more important. Finding workable keys to life's second half and pushing through doors to new possibilities, coupled with perseverance and determination, helped make middle life manageable, ministers said.

The apostle Paul, in his epistle to the church in Philippi, wrote of rejoicing in the Lord and praising the day's good despite negative circumstances and weighty baggage. Sometimes that is all we can do; sometimes we have to touch the brink, the edge—be tested and tried—to see salvation, the hope, and new beginnings. Paul was not fearful, for he found the good and praised it. "I eagerly expect and hope that I will in no way be ashamed, but will have sufficient courage so that now as always Christ will be exalted in my body, whether by life or by death" (Philippians 1:20 NIV).

The pastors I encountered used a number of solutions to ease this transitional phase. Some played golf, while others insisted on long-scheduled contractual vacations (something that elder pastors were rarely able to do during their time). Some have incorporated serious exercise regimens into their daily routines, and others have found a variety of creative outlets.

A few years ago, I started painting, creating on canvas what I could not express emotionally, could not speak, and could not convey in other ways. Something transformative happened when colors blended, patterns formed, and images I had thought about only subconsciously came together. It was a release. I committed to bettering my health, which meant cutting back hours, napping, listening to my aging and sometimes aching body, being practical about the number of speaking engagements I accepted, and delegating more ministry responsibilities to my very capable staff. I had been training them for that purpose, and now, for my own sustainability, I needed to trust them and my years of guidance. Stepping away is not always an easy task.

Another pastor with whom I spoke told me in an attempt to escape the rigors of his church and family life, he took flying lessons. He found the experience freeing and liberating, and now he flies as much as he can.

Then another preacher echoed the suggestion I have consistently made to all pastors within the sound of my voice: therapy, the ultimate secure place for the unburdening of one's personal stuff. This particular well-educated and articulate theologian, Hasani, avails himself of the opportunity on a weekly basis.

"Men are like car glove compartments," Hasani said. "To get to our owner's manuals, to reach the heart of who we are, we have to open the glove compartment and move all the stuff out of the way to find the keys. The problem is, we do not move the stuff very often, and we don't want to give someone else the keys because that is tantamount to sharing all of our weaknesses and vulnerabilities. If I give you that manual or the keys, you know my failings, and you might exploit them. Not everyone should have access to your private spaces and private thoughts. Most people should only have valet keys, and a few should have master keys."

He continued, "As pastors, many of us find ourselves in trouble because we hand out too many sets of those masters—many times to women. This is why the anonymity of the therapy process is so incredibly powerful. You don't necessarily have to care if your thoughts are organized, or if they go off in a particular direction. You can just empty out all of who you are and not worry. It is a selfish engagement and a self-serving process in many ways, but one that is necessary and needed."

Hasani described his desire to see the development of a true men-only pastors' gathering where failures and fears could be honestly tackled in an atmosphere of spiritual support and healing, shepherded by respected elder theologians who could guide, direct, and share, making sure conversations did not go "off the rails."

He said having a sacred space is important because the other side of the "valet key" scenario is the burden of familiarity and having to discard the mask ministers don every day. "We need somewhere to talk about the stuff we aren't supposed to talk about," Hasani said. "The real and authentic, the affair, the unsatisfactory marriage and sex life, the ungrateful congregation and declining budget stuff—pastors are human, with human needs and desires."

To work through my own midlife challenges, I have taken the opportunity to travel around the country conducting workshops for ministers on post-pastoral transitions, clergy sexuality, and personal responsibility. It has been an education for me and for those to whom I have spoken. In those workshops, I address a number of topics, but most important for men at or near the half-century mark has been finding a modicum of joy and happiness, and making the conscious decision to do so.

The Bible says, "The joy of the LORD is your strength" (Nehemiah 8:10 NIV). Laughter and contentment are signs of joy and satisfaction, and sometimes we simply have to "fake it until we make it." Truthfully, as overachievers and men committed to the gospel, many of us take our profession and ourselves entirely too seriously.

Praise and laughter need to be a part of our daily walk, as well as the contemplative aspects of a "religious" life.

Although these suggestions may sound pedestrian, they work, not only for midlife and ministers, but also for any man or person on a journey. Start with reexamining personal boundaries and relationships, especially those with whom "master keys" are frequently exchanged. I will say it again: work on giving parishioners the whole of God, but not the whole of you. Is a church policy in place to hold you and your staff accountable for questionable behaviors? Is there a long-term planning committee examining options for various succession plans? What is your escape valve to release the day's pressure? Who is the keeper of your secrets—your "stuff"—with whom you share what God already knows, and are you confident when morning comes, your life will not be headline news? Is there a person you can call in total confidence and lay your burdens bare?

Practice compassion; do not just preach it. Stories of fallen and besieged leaders, from pastors to politicians, are as old as Sarah and Abraham when they gave birth to Isaac. Instead of playing a lively game of late-night preacher gossip, help to restore and resurrect our colleagues when they misstep, for we never know if a time will come when our spouse decides she is done, or when a bottle of tequila calls our name after years of sobriety, or when our church votes "no confidence," or when our health fails.

We have to awaken each day to our own reflections, believing that God has God's hands on us, knowing we were born to serve God's people, and that midlife is merely a phase. We have to confront our demons and chart new courses. To not do so means we are running aimlessly in circles, out of breath, never finding the meaning for which we searched. We do not want to be disqualified for the prize God promised. We want our latter days to be our better days, and we want those days to have value and meaning.

Holocaust survivor and Austrian neurologist and psychiatrist Viktor E. Frankl wrote in his pivotal book, *Man's Search for Meaning*, that for most of us, "meaning" is an elusive something we must come to terms with in good and bad situations in order to move forward and to make a difference. "When we are no longer able to change a situation, we are challenged to change ourselves. . . . In some ways suffering ceases to be suffering at the moment it finds a meaning, such as the meaning of a sacrifice."[2]

This path is not an easy one. But with sacrifice, direction, and planning, the midlife trek can be made manageable. We have to listen to ourselves, not turn a deaf ear to the voice of God, and not be afraid to reach beyond our comfort zones.

When I started sharing my story, sure, some folks thought, "I knew that Donald Hilliard was crazy." More people, though, have found ways to share with me a personal anecdote and a tale they had not told. Surely, if God has helped me through my struggles with an expanding church, grown daughters leaving their overprotective daddy, and repairing a long-term drifting marriage, God will take care of someone else. We need, as our ancestors so often sang about, the "wonder-working power" of Jesus, the blood he shed, for he is the one who can and will carry us through our present circumstances. We must make conscious decisions to thrive and survive, which can be determined only by applied spiritual discipline. Our goal should be to find whatever constructive outlets work and allow us to hold on and hold out through rough times until we can arrive safely on the other side of our pain.

We do not want to miss the voice of God because we are stuck in the messiness of our own minutiae. So we have to commit to the Lord that we will change or hearts, our attitudes, and our minds. We will say yes to God's will and to God's way. We will say no to all that has us bound and captured. We have to accept there will be good days and bad days, knowing God is in control, so we should not complain, because we can do all things through Christ, who strengthens us. We have the power to change our circumstances and get through this journey. Our change will come.

Midlife Discussions

1. How do you plan to change directions in an effort to create authenticity in your family, church, and personal life to help you transition through your midlife phase?

2. When you rip the Band-Aid off, what will the wound look like? What was it covering: lack of faith, insecurity, infidelity, or alcoholism? How do you plan to shift gears and plan for a new personal walk with God?

3. What is your theology of hope? What keeps you dry and steady when the rains come?

4. What is your new plan of action to save yourself and your church when the floods come the next time?

Notes

1. Gardner C. Taylor, *Faith in the Fire: Wisdom for Life* (New York: SmileyBooks, 2011), 63.

2. Viktor E. Frankl, *Man's Search for Meaning* (New York: Pocket Books, 1959), 135.

8

Forgiveness, Responsibility, and Restoration — Next Steps

Create in me a pure heart, O God, and renew a steadfast spirit within me. Do not cast me from your presence or take your Holy Spirit from me.
                    —Psalm 51:10-11 NIV

"Hurt people hurt people." That is one of those well-seasoned adages all us have heard. In the second half of our ministerial lives and during our midlife experiences, whether we are contemplating retirement, working on succession planning, releasing a negative or inappropriate relationship, dismissing a cantankerous choir director, or preserving our legacies, part of the healing process must begin with forgiveness of self, releasing past regrets, and a renewal of the spirit to make room for new blessings from God.

Psalm 51 is an all-encompassing song and public prayer of forgiveness, written by David after his affair with Bathsheba. It is interesting how we keep returning to David and this particular Scripture, perhaps because it speaks perfectly to midlife angst. There was not a single pastor interviewed for this book who did not refer to this passage in some manner, explicitly or implicitly.

It is Scripture filled with regret and sorrow, but also it is an open request, more like a plea, actually, for forgiveness of self and from God. David does not want to be cast from the light of God's grace and favor. He is a grown man, powerful and fully aware of his transgressions, the sins against self and the Holy Father. For most of us, preachers and otherwise, we "get" David. We can relate. We have been there more times than most of us care to openly admit.

But if we are truthful and honest with ourselves, by the time we comb gray hair and reach the very last notch on our belts, most of us have made a mess of a relationship or two, with our families, with church elders, stewards, and the search committee we didn't know had been convened. We are human and extremely fallible. We know the good news of Jesus Christ; we preach it and teach it, but at times we have difficulty living it. God, though, forgives and knows all about our troubles. One of my favorite hymns of the church speaks to this:

> There's not a Friend like the lowly Jesus:
> No, not one! No, not one!
> No one else could heal all our souls' diseases:
> No, not one! No, not one!
> Jesus knows all about our struggles;
> He will guide 'til the day is done:
> There's not a Friend like the lowly Jesus:
> No, not one! No, not one!
> —Johnson Oatman, Jr., 1895, No Not One

Step One: Take Responsibility

We cannot make the next move or take the next step, walk a new walk, find true respite and retreat, or expect God's bountiful rewards unless and until we ask forgiveness and—wait for it—and forgive ourselves. To receive the forgiveness we seek, we have to accept responsibility for past behaviors, whatever they may be. Accepting our faults does not mean we are not talented and excellent examples of God's creation. Many of us no longer want to own our choices and the consequences that result. Forgiveness happens when an act of contrition takes place and we have acknowledged our shortcomings. These are difficult tasks. It is, as I have been attempting to convey, a journey. The God we serve is a God of hope and a God of second chances. We all need an opportunity to try again.

One pastor told me that after a brief but serious battle with alcoholism and an extended period of loneliness, inappropriate attraction to women in his congregation, and an acute crisis of faith, he had a "come to Jesus" moment and realized he "could have a life outside ministry and outside the church." Though tested, he did not waver; his love for the Lord remained unchanged. He did, though, begin to think about the possibility of retirement, so he made certain that church bylaws reflected his desire to prepare for an eventual transition when he decided he was ready. But to get to that point, he knew damage had to be repaired, forgiveness of sin accepted, and a recommitment to his faith needed to be made. Ultimately, he had to find healthier ways to manage middle age. "Have mercy on me, O God, according to your unfailing love; according to your great compassion blot out my transgressions" (Psalm 51:1 NIV).

The lessons learned—forgiveness from God, forgiveness of self, and forgiveness of persons affected and offended—are necessary for a transformative experience. We cannot change the past, but we can redirect and recreate better futures by tending to neglected relationships and broken churches and developing a better sense of personal responsibility by being accountable for our actions. Yes, aging is daunting, and we do not talk about it as much as we need to. It is a sensitive, secretive, and ego-draining thing, but we do not have to give in or give up. It does not have to become a dramatic movie cliché where someone gets exploited, a scandal ensues, a bad ending follows, the screen fades to black, and credits roll.

Matthew 7 records Jesus saying we should examine ourselves and our motives and refrain from criticizing in others what is often the very thing we despise in ourselves. Faith can and will carry us through those valleys. Faith can allow midlife to be a time of introspection, reflection, and true spiritual inventory.

Step Two: Confront Fear

One of the pastors I mentored wrote his midlife story in an unpublished document, which he shared with me, called "The Truth About Me." He wrote of his journey to find what was true for him in the private space that he rarely exposed to anyone. He finally revealed that most of his interactions with parishioners and those he encountered had been based on falsities and a self-created "other" he had created. No one really knew his story and the truth of his pain until he made a decision to forgive himself and make a change. "My first step in telling the truth was to stop lying to myself and to start confessing what was really true about my life," he said. "Pride for me was probably the main reason for living a life that was true to others but a lie to me. I had become fearful of what people would say if they knew I was in need of deliverance more than they were."

Fear is what keeps most of us bound, constrained, and stuck in the ugliness of our "stuff." We fear change, getting older, losing our reputations and the respect of our congregations and communities. We fear secrets surfacing and insecurities becoming visible. Ultimately, we fear that those we cover will see who really we are, and that we fall and fail more often than we stand and succeed. As pastors, we know the power of the spoken word and how words affect the listener. All of us have come in contact with that person who uses the gift of speech to talk his or her way into or out of almost any situation. Well, use that same power to get yourself through "the troubles," be they midlife or something else. Talk yourself into deliverance, into healing, and into joy. Take responsibility, trust God, declare hope, and celebrate victory; and then, encourage yourself. "Trust in the LORD with all your heart and lean not on your own understanding; in all your ways submit to him, and he will make your paths straight" (Proverbs 3:5-6 NIV).

Step Three: Choose Right Paths

While it is undoubtedly true that many of the problems we encounter in midlife are the result of inexorable forces, it is also true many issues are of our own creation. So how do we make a comeback and find restoration? How do we heal from our unholy hiccups, and what are our next steps? After accepting responsibility and acknowledging our fears, we must recognize where we are on the journey and decide where we want that path to lead.

Although we are pastors and we minister to others, do we pray as faithfully and fervently as we should? I mentioned earlier we spend so much of our time giving; we often neglect who we are and who we thought ourselves to be. If we are spiritually dead and cannot move forward, then progress will never happen. Light a fire in your soul. God cannot light the candle in your heart if you have no wick. Remember how to pray: not just by rote and how we were taught in seminary, but by hurt and through heart. Sing praises and remember this: we have been through this before, and God never fails. God abides and gives victory to those who seek it.

One of the beauties of the African American worship experience is our music; it is open and warm, full-bodied and engaging, enhancing the preached word in a unique and powerful way. Numerous hymn writers and musicians have penned music about God's faithfulness to broken people, for each and every one of us is a shattered vessel—cracked, battered, and in need of repair. But there is hope. There is healing, and there is restoration. Famed gospel musician Walter Hawkins penned a song, "The Potter's House," based on Scripture from Jeremiah, which speaks to the repair all of us need as broken vessels and shattered souls in search of salvation. God told the prophet Jeremiah, "Go down to the potter's house, and there I will give you my message." And Jeremiah responded: "So I went down to the potter's house, and I saw him working at the wheel. But the pot he was shaping from the clay was marred in his hands; so the potter formed it into another pot, shaping it as seemed best to him" (Jeremiah 18:2-4 NIV).

Step Four: Pursue Restoration

Repairing ourselves—putting back the pieces of our ministries, tattered relationships, battered self-esteems, and injured spirits—is healing and restorative, and it puts us on the path to pondering what comes next and engaging in a the possibility of a future. The process of repair, the therapy, and the mending that must take place in midlife sets the stage for a clean slate, a new blank board on which to mark new goals and aspirations. So on to the future.

I have often thought of myself a coach to young pastors in the faith who need guidance and direction. I see mentoring as a way of helping the next generation to avoid personal and ministerial mishaps, to help them become effective community leaders and men of principle. If we stay occupied with good works and gifts of the heart, we will not have time for a midlife crisis or stress-related breakdowns, bright red sports cars, girlfriends half our age, and doubts about our chosen vocation to serve the Lord our God. On second thought, the sports car just might be acceptable!

Restoration and next steps: "Cleanse me with hyssop, and I will be clean; wash me, and I will be whiter than snow" (Psalm 51:7 NIV). Each Sunday morning we stand before the faithful and proclaim good news to those gathered in sanctuaries across the country who are waiting for an uplifting word from the pastor. Whether we have been inspired by the Holy Spirit, or angered by a spouse, or had too much to drink the night before, or the world was simply too much with us, we endeavor to give congregants what they seek: good news. Worthy or not, faults and all, warts aplenty, we rise and give God the greatest glory.

We all worship the same God, the one who brought Shadrach, Meshach, and Abednego out of an inferno; the same God who parted the Red Sea for the children of Israel and rained manna from the heavens for them to eat; the same God who raised Jesus from the dead. If the God we serve is that mighty, surely that God can move us successfully through the trials of midlife and past the shame and regret of our transgressions. "The LORD is my shepherd, I shall not want. He makes me lie down in green pastures; he leads me beside the still waters; he restores my soul. He leads me in right paths for his name's sake" (Psalm 23:1-3 NRSV).

The word of God still works. We can be renewed, revived, and transformed. God has our backs. We have to believe the words we preach, and we have to be held to a higher standard of behavior. No one said this journey would be a road easily traveled or one without condemnation. We are going to fall and fail, but we have to get up and try again. As pastors and as men, we do the "I got this" thing when help and hope are just a prayer and another brother preacher a phone call away. Hurt people know hurt people, and broken vessels need repair. So we must plan next steps, trust, move past doubts, and hold fast to convictions.

Each pastor I interviewed moved through a process of healing and becoming whole with some sort of assistance either from outside professional help or from turning to a trusted person in order to master whatever had him bound. We cannot find restoration on our own. We cannot take next steps without someone on whom to lean. And we cannot bandage brokenness without an appropriate salve. As musicians through the ages, from anonymous Negro spiritual writers of old to contemporary gospel artists of today have said and sung, we must be healed. There is healing for our souls because there is still a balm in Gilead.

Midlife Discussions

1. Do you have a real and consistent prayer life? Many of us get so caught up in ministering to others that we forget ourselves and our training—the thing keeping us on the right path. How can you start your restoration by renewing your own relationship with the power of prayer?

2. Guilt can be a self-destructive emotion, one that slowly eats away at the fabric of who we are, shifting relationship, altering perspective. What do you feel guilty about?

3. Forgiveness can allow you to release the past, to move through pain to begin anew. It is a start. Have you begun to forgive yourself? Why or why not?

4. What are your next steps, and how do you plan to get there?

9

Where Do We Go from Here?

I press on toward the goal to win the prize for which God
has called me heavenward in Christ Jesus.
—Philippians 3:14 NIV

"Where do we go from here?" That question seems to find
its way into the socio-religious fabric of every generation.
How do we piece our lives together in a way that not only
mends and renews our spirits, but also enhances our ministries and personal lives? What will help us make peace
with those mistakes that we acknowledge and the King
David-like sins we hide in darkness, even from ourselves?
How do we get to a place of safety, a place of comfort, so
we can minister not only to ourselves but also to those we
are called to serve? *So, where do we go from here?*

In 1967, at the Southern Christian Leadership Conference in Atlanta, Georgia, Rev. Dr. Martin Luther King Jr.
said in order to answer the question "Where do we go from
here," with any amount of honesty and integrity, we must
recognize fully the state and nature of where we are currently. In other words, first we have to know where "here" is.
Only then can we figure out where to go next and the proper direction in which we should head.

Midlife is often a stark and lonely place. When we are compelled to answer midlife's call and the question "Where is here?" the subsequent inquiry can be more than daunting. Yes, midlife is a concrete reminder we "ain't what we used to be"—those days of being the high school wrestling and football star are gone. Maybe even the sports car we talked about in earlier days seems a tad silly, and that pipe dream is not hitting the spot that you thought it would. The good news is you still have the same saving grace of God's good news—the gospel—and *there* is where you should lean and find strength, not false pillars, past and present, that have failed you. God still can use you, and God still has plans for your life beyond a particular season of suffering.

So where do you go from here? The choice is yours. You make the plans, guided by God's power and led by the Holy Spirit. You decide. Several of the preachers I interviewed and talked with along the way simply made choices to change or not to change, and each decision came with a set of costs and consequences. But each man of God made a choice, and then he either had to live with the threat of public scandals or he created a situation where he did the hard work needed to make a better tomorrow and to heal.

It seems that not a day goes by when you cannot turn on CNN or MSNBC and hear about another brother preacher who is caught up, or caught in, what has to be midlife crisis. From being accused of attempting to drive a Bentley over a church's First Lady, to being arrested for allegedly abusing a teenage daughter—whatever the issue, the choices, behaviors, and lives of preachers are being monitored, not only by the God we serve, but also by an eager, rapid-response, 24/7 media machine. Yes, we are all mortal, and in our humanness we fall short—every day. For those of us who are supposed to be role models, we must not let our low points and our closet skeletons define our ministries, our mission, or our message.

Every preacher who took significant risk and told me his story did so to help another brother push past his midlife crisis and chart a different course. That is what my personal therapist would call the development of next steps—making a decision to let things become, not a mess, but a memory—of new discovery and a challenging period of time, managed because you had a purpose and a plan. As a man of God, your first step is to recognize that people can be served and saved, but not at the neglect and expense of your well-being and soul. Empire building—the state of continual acquisition—is only as solid and productive as the theological foundation on which it is being constructed.

Take time to assess the firmness of your foundation. Are your members being adequately fed with spiritual nourishment? Do you have the kind of relationship with God that you preach to others? Teach others how to fortify themselves against their issues and follow said advice. Admit to yourself and to God that you are not perfect, that you are merely a broken vessel in need of healing and wholeness. Do not be so invested in the church's next building phase, or anxious about who can be invited to the church's annual lecture series, or concerned with what another preacher might claim to be constructing. Concentrate on cleaning up your own emotional fortress and physical house. Sweep away the clutter and look for a safe place to reflect. Focus on what is at hand and work to improve it. And above all, lean on Jesus, remembering God is a mighty fortress and the foundation of all your training and your faith, and that of the ancestors.

So, again, how firm is your foundation? And, where do we go from here?

The next step is to set attainable and realistic goals. Your purpose is the object toward which you strive. "Many are the plans in a person's heart, but it is the LORD's purpose that prevails" (Proverbs 19:21 NIV). Setting new and bigger goals is as important as creating healthy new outlets to express yourself. Such outlets may include exploring new hobbies, traveling, establishing a consistent exercise routine, making an unbreakable date night with your spouse—anything that helps to redirect and establish safe patterns of behavior. Set purposeful and attainable goals, not just lofty dreams that are out of reach. Life has numerous pitfalls, period. And in midlife, the choices we make and have made can play catch-up with us. So, decisions must be made either to maneuver through creative crises or to remain satisfied with comfortable complacency. Yes, we can get lost and lose our way, stuck in our own "stuff." What's optimal, though, is retreating, regrouping, retraining, and relearning, so eventually there is progress and positive movement ahead.

Where do we go from here? Know first that God still can use us and still has plans. Decide whether you are simply going to live, or whether you are going to live well in the will of God. Three key principles have helped me get through this journey, and I hope they will work for you as well.

First, move out of your own way and reestablish personal relationships. Reestablish these relationships with Christ, your spouse, your family, and then with friends. As men of the gospel, many of us have few friends. We are used to serving people and having people serve us, but often we do not work to create real and abiding friendships. Once we have connected to God, we can touch those in our midst, and we can touch and agree with our neighbors.

All of these restored and renewed relationships have a healing impact because we move the focus outside of ourselves and beyond the midlife confusion. If we do that, we will discover that we are not alone in our pain, our confusion, or our joy, for each one of us is bruised, broken, and battered. We are communal beings, so we need each other to heal and find solace and to survive.

Second, be intentional about praying. My church members know that I believe in consistent and deliberate prayer; it is our lifeline. Prayer changes outcomes and circumstances. No wonder, then, the apostle Paul exhorts us to pray and lift holy hands without anger or quarreling (1 Timothy 2:8).

Third, find the good and praise it. Be positive. Do you view your situation as a blessing or as a curse? An article on the MSNBC website entitled "The Recession's Biggest Victims: The Great Recession Could Well Be Known as the 'Black Mancession'" painted a disturbing picture of the plight of men, particularly African American men, in securing gainful employment. The article reported a 17 percent unemployment rate among African American men, double the rate for Caucasian males. That number was publicly reported, and so in actuality the number may be much higher. Those are cold hard facts, and we live with such realities every day. All of us need a prophetic disposition, a positive attitude, and an optimistic perspective, even in the face of harsh truths.

There are those in ministerial garb who think me naïve. And maybe I am. I do know that there are enormous pressures in ministry and during midlife, with the shedding of old skin, morphing anew, and relearning different ways to manage weaknesses. Attending to the needs of a people while trying to find a place to decompress and be who you are can be overwhelming. There are home pressures, car troubles, kid issues, renovations, tuitions, and other concerns. Add those things to the combustible and emotional experience of male midlife—something that most men do not want to talk about anyway—and you have an explosive powder keg. So, really, where do we go from here?

As leaders, we are called each week to bring a relevant and meaningful word from the Lord. But our personal issues are ever before us. All of us have something we are dealing with, but our flawed human proclivities do not have to become the undoing of our calling to proclaim the gospel of Jesus Christ. We absorb the pain of others, and we must let go of our own to heal and make a true difference. That happens through trust. We have to trust the spouse God put in our lives, the training we have received, and the God and faith of our ancestors.

We cannot cross midlife's threshold without trust. We have to able to trust the promises of God, the word of the Lord, and the Spirit of God, who brings calm assurance. Where there is trust, there is no room for fear, and if there is no room for fear, there is only space for love and light to abide. Some of us have forgotten how to lean on God's unchanging hand. Some of us have forgotten how to build our hope on things that will last. Some of us preach on Sunday morning, but we have forgotten truly how to spend time with God. Instead, we become self-destructive and insular. We turn to one who makes us feel better in the still of the night, and whether that one is a shapely, easy-on-the-eyes woman or a decorative glass bottle full of brandy, both lead to the same thing: regret.

So how about spending time with the God of our weary years—the God of Martin L. King Jr., Sojourner Truth, Gardner C. Taylor, Benjamin E. Mays, Fannie Lou Hamer, Henry H. Mitchell, Samuel B. McKinney, Wyatt T. Walker, and Jeremiah A. Wright Jr. The God who worked and continues to work through those men and women can also work through us. The psalmist said, "I was young and now I am old, yet I have never seen the righteous forsaken or their children begging bread" (Psalm 37:25 NIV).

Where do we go from here? From here, we must be willing to cross the threshold and trust. Today we must trust that God is able to keep us from falling when we feel as if the pressures of life will take us under. God is able to be a friend when it seems as if our spouse no longer knows us. God is able to help us recover our dreams. God will recover it all. God is able to be our guide. In the name of Jesus, we have the victory!

Midlife Discussions
1. What is your plan of action to overcome your struggle?
2. What impact has your midlife experience had on relationships between you and your loved ones?
3. How do you involve your partner in your coping process or healing process?

10

May the Circle Be Unbroken

What Jesus did here in Cana of Galilee was the first of the signs through which he revealed his glory; and his disciples believed in him.

—John 2:11 NIV

In many ways, the midlife circle for me was complete on August 7, 2010. That was my youngest daughter's wedding day. The night before the big event, our last night together in the house as this particular configuration of a family unit, my wife and I asked if she would sleep with her parents one last time, like back in the day, when we would cuddle up because of an impending storm, a bad day at school, or just because. On that particular night we were certainly aware we needed her far more than she ever needed us. I pulled her head to my heart and hugged her tightly. I knew it would not be the last father-daughter special moment, but I did not want it to end. Our baby girl, the unexpected blessing, the youngest and the last, was getting married and would soon be presented to the love of her life.

My midlife expeditions started when I acknowledged the incredibly paralyzing fear I felt when watching my daughters leave our home, one by one. Although their departures were reasonable, anticipated, and expected—for college and the stuff of life—each one triggered a series of transitions, crises actually that I had to manage, work through, and find coping strategies to survive—such as simply focusing on breathing—so I could continue to be productive in my home life and in my ministry. I had just become used to the idea I was no longer the young, energetic man I wanted to be and thought I was. I had mourned, buried, and accepted his figurative death, and now I was to give away my baby girl. I hit my internal rewind button, and then I went for the master switch and pushed reset. "Breathe," I said to myself. "Here we go again. Breathe. Just breathe."

I have been doing diligent and consistent work on the topic of midlife, manhood, and ministry transitions, preaching and teaching across the country, telling my story and taking other pastors into my confidence. And now this little girl, my child, the last one of my three, was trying to challenge all my work by seriously leaving and getting married. Of course I knew, once again, I was being unreasonable, but Lord knows I wondered what I had done wrong and where I went off course. I prayed, I cried, and I was (as many fathers on the planet are initially) ridiculously irrational when first hearing about a young man wanting to marry my baby. Now it was her wedding day, and all things, midlife and otherwise, truly had come full circle.

The morning of the wedding went flawlessly well. The girls had their hair done, pictures were taken, and my wife and I were satisfied we had planned a day for a princess bride. As we stood near the front door, watching our youngest descend the spiral staircase dressed in her wedding gown, I thought of all the happiness she and her sisters have given us. When we arrived at the church and exited the limousine, I thanked God for allowing me the opportunity to experience this incredible moment. Ultimately, I was indeed pleased with the man she had chosen. My father's days had been numbered, but God granted me favor, and I was present, alive, for this moment.

I have been struck in so many ways by this midlife process, by what we go through as men in ministry—the pits and peaks, the mountains high and valleys low—and how we struggle with the statistical outcomes and battle plans. We fall, fail, and get back up. That activity is one repeated on a daily basis, like an endless, looping, mental cassette tape. (Being old school, I still have one of those ancient, audio recordings playing in my head!)

I recall these days with good humor, some regret, and affection, but I also realize that letting go and letting God and learning to be flexible have been a significant part of the midlife journey. And while learning to be flexible, we must also remember to utilize the power of prayer and praise. The psalmist wrote, "I will bless the LORD at all times; his praise shall continually be in my mouth. . . . O magnify the LORD with me, and let us exalt his name together. I sought the LORD, and he answered me, and delivered me from all my fears. . . . O taste and see that the LORD is good" (Psalm 34:1, 3-4, 8 NRSV).

I had to remind myself that in moments of heightened anxiety and a little inflexibility, like when a beloved daughter gets married, I must not lose the power found in personal prayer. God makes an appearance when we make a commitment to praise and pray without ceasing. Yes, we are men of the gospel, but often we are so focused on helping others find their salvation that we neglect our own. Yes, midlife can be a confusing phase with whirlwinds of activity, church transitions, uncharted territories, and major adjustments that involve figuring out what that newly shaped life looks like and how it will feel, and holding on to the faith we teach others are primary keys to getting through difficult moments. Simple but true, basic and pedestrian, but sometimes the most brilliant solutions are.

So I walked my daughter down the aisle, lifted her veil, and kissed her forehead, both cheeks, and rubbed her nose with mine, as I have done since she was a baby—then I let go. I let her go. Earlier, I had a private moment of tears and complete loss of composure, but I shook it off and joined my wife as our princess united with her prince. I was breathing. God truly is mighty and powerful.

Midlife does not have to be miserable, and there is hope beyond all of our "stuff"—our pulpits and congregations, our transgressions and peccadilloes. There is life outside the next problem a church member has; there is life beyond our fears and our regrets, beyond our should-haves, could-haves, wants, and wishes. It is obvious that my wife and I made our daughters the centers of our joy. But the favors that all of us have been granted—our churches, our spouses and children, and our positions as leaders in the community—are only on temporary loan from God. The reality is that midlife transitions, by text-book definition, mean that things will change.

That is what plodding through midlife, manhood, and ministry entails; it is the working characterization of the experience. Responsibilities still reign supreme. We are still responsible, but those duties take on a different shape, texture, and feel. Our grown children are capable because we raised them. At some point we simply must let go and prepare to share our beloved son or daughter with someone else, and with the world. Our children will leave, no matter how much it shatters our hearts, so we need to take that opportunity to reconnect with our spouses, clean up broken relationships, cut off inappropriate connections, develop well-planned exit strategies, and create new futures. Giving a child away in marriage is merely one step in that direction.

Being flexible now simply goes with the territory. The pulpit will not crumble without our presence or the sound of our voice projecting through a specially crafted microphone. Ministry is and has always been a 24/7/365 round-the-clock job. Yes, Jesus worked non-stop saving souls until the moment he hung between two thieves and ascended to his Father—but we are not Jesus. We know that intellectually, but many of us suffer from the Lazarus syndrome. We think we can raise the dead, and we must be all things to all people, when at this time and in this moment we simply need to ride the wave of readjustment, clean up the past, and enjoy the process of change. We work hard, and we should play just as hard. Most of us do not take that time. I am a work in progress, for that is a lesson I am still learning.

A popular pastor told me that when he prepared for retirement and succession planning, it had been a long-term and involved process, and he contemplated a variety of things. Should he continue to attend church on a weekly basis? Should he move out of the city where he pastored? How would the new pastor be received? How should special services, honorariums, and a plethora of other important church and pastoral-related issues be handled? But the one thing he was sure of and had no second thoughts about was that it was time to retire and pass the torch to another capable pastor, to enjoy his own family, to write and read, and to appreciate God's bounty.

Although I am not retiring right now (I am still paying for graduate school tuition!) I would be shading the truth if I said I was not planning for succession. As a bishop, I cover many young pastors in the ministry. I have a number of talented ministers at Cathedral International today who help make sure ministry gets done in our various locations, from our weekly services, to our multiple conferences, to engagements across the country. I am planning for the future, for midlife, ministry, and beyond. My daughters may have prompted this midlife path, but with God's grace, prayer, and preparation, I intend on following where it leads: as in the great old hymn by Ernest Blandy, "Where he leads me I will follow; where he leads me I will follow; I'll go with him, with him, all the way."

In this season, I am asking God to look beyond my faults and see my needs. And I am asking Jesus to be a fence around my fears because I do not want my midlife manhood stuff to get in the way of all the good that is occurring. I am truly looking forward to this next phase, whatever it will be. My oldest daughter completed graduate school and started her career. Our middle daughter finished college and is in graduate school, and our youngest has also finished college and also is in graduate school, as is her husband. Those are blessings. My wife is now working on her master's degree in seminary after years of raising our children. I've taught at Palmer and New Brunswick Theological Seminaries, guest lectured at Howard University Divinity School, and most recently collaborated with famed theologian Leonard Sweet in a new DMin concentration at Drew University. I was excited about those opportunities. My father's life ended at the age of fifty-three, in the prime of midlife, but with God's anointing power, I look forward to living well beyond and exceeding all expectations. My goal is to be like Abraham and live to "a good old age" (Genesis 15:15 NIV).

I am blessed beyond measure. I have a faithful and committed church, a loving wife, three lovely daughters, and a renewed sense of self. I am mastering midlife and turning a page to be a new word in the world, for midlife does not have to be a complicated puzzle. The words on these pages are merely suggestions, meditations, and shared stories of struggle and success that I leave as a guide for another's personal journey. They are my stories and the stories of others who bravely told their own tales. I pray that something has resonated with you and can be the beginning of a special, sacred blueprint created and designed for your own successful transition through midlife, manhood, and ministry—and beyond.

Say, "yes!" and be healed.

Afterword

The inner life of African American men has been a matter of myth, stereotype, conjecture, and race-based cultural bias as well as condemnation.

For those of us in Christian ministry, the too-often self-imposed and congregational need for us to project an impenetrable strength and "superhero" emotional stamina mitigates against our human need for counsel, stress relief, and therapy. Quite frankly, until recently even "educated" African American men have been resistant to any suggestion of personal mental health intervention. Unfortunately, this has included marriage counseling.

Consequently, the very notion of male "midlife crisis" is not a matter that has been broached by African American clergy, whether in ministry or in our personal lives. Several years ago my wife, who is also an ordained minister in the AME Church, shared with me that while the culture spends a great deal of time and resources addressing women and their midlife changes and experiences, the midlife crises of men often go unacknowledged and unreported. In this volume Bishop Donald Hilliard faces this issue head-on.

As a clergyman I am pleased that Bishop Hilliard has given this work added meaning and a sharper focus by dealing with the effect this midlife journey can and does have on ministers, their families, and their churches. Bishop Hilliard does a masterful job in addressing midlife issues so many men experience but find difficult to share with others. Because women tend to talk in a more open way about their feelings, they are often frustrated with the men in their lives who are unwilling to hold such conversations. What many women miss is the reason men are not open to discuss feelings: men find it difficult to share their emotions.

Bishop Hilliard deals with the midlife issues that come from a man's perspective. He is very helpful in leading men into this much-needed conversation by being completely transparent as it relates to his own life.

Those of us who are in ministry do not receive a "hall pass" in living out of our manhood. Bishop Hilliard reveals that men in ministry are not exempt from the challenges that come with marriage, parenting, and aging. Our experiences can be further complicated by the unhealthy denial of problems in our personal lives. Many are further saddled with guilt and shame as it relates to our issues.

Bishop Hilliard creates a safe and spiritually therapeutic path for us to begin our healing. His step-by-step approach will benefit anyone ready to deal positively with matters of midlife, manhood, and ministry. I genuinely believe this book will be helpful for all men as well as for women who want to better understand the men in their lives.

I pray you will be as blessed as I have been.

—Bishop John R. Bryant, DMin
Senior Bishop and Presiding Prelate
Fourth Episcopal District of the
African Methodist Episcopal Church